Dear Terry, ple...

CW00418439

BEATRICE SHI
A DAME WITH DE

BORN IN 1909 SHE SAVED OUR PILOTS IN WWII. GAINED A GOLD
STAR AT BROOKLANDS RACING BIKES & CARS AT 100MPH! WAS A
STEM PIONEER BEFORE HER TIME WHILE FIGHTING FOR EQUALITY
IN A MAN'S WORLD. BEATRICE *TILLY* SHILLING DID IT ALL!

ELSIE O'NEILL

**Flying over-head is a Spitfire.
The Overlord Celebrations and Military Display
in Denmead, Waterlooville, are remembering
Victory over Japan in 1945 and other Wars.
A fitting day for me to complete this book and remember Beatrice, a
local girl of grit, spirit & determination.**

*A well-researched record telling how one young girl was determined
to follow her dream and succeed in a male dominated world. An
encouragement for all girls so inclined to pursue a STEM career.*

David Woodford, Beatrice's nephew
February 2021

*Elsie O'Neill x
(aka Melody)*

COPYRIGHT

ISBN: 9798493758638

BALLYCOPELAND BOOKS UK

Cover Design: Izabeladesign

elsieoneillauthor@g.mail.com

http://ballycopelandbooks.uk

Praise for
Beatrice Shilling OBE:
A Dame with Determination!

Women have always been powerful, but men tended to write history and forget about the contribution females made to our world. Determination is what kept them going and Beatrice certainly showed what women can do in man's world. She is amazing – from racing cars and bikes to saving the lives of our airmen in WWII.

Men have a lot to answer for, then and now!

Tony Ashridge *Author*

****

Written in a very clear and easy to read manner exploring her love of bikes, fast cars and the need to succeed at all costs. Amazing photographs supplement the text which goes a long way to showing how Beatrice worked exhaustingly hard to gain the success she deserved.

I love the modern outlook on STEM and how sad that gender issues in science, technology, engineering and maths were an issue 100 years ago and still are today! *Such a disgrace in 2021.* Make a move to change that, girls and boys!

A.P.B. *Single Mum, Teacher and modern feminist*

****

It hits the mark in many ways. Introducing different subjects such as International Women's Day – I didn't know there was one! Also the former Brooklands racing track, now a place of expertise for STEM enthusiasts and much more makes sound reading for both knowledge and interest.

The superb photographs, the background information with a few notes on B's family history as well as excellent text make it a comfortable read, pulling you in without being too heavy on the history side, yet gets several messages across.

Equality for all is essential, but importantly you can succeed with determination, hard work and building on those first steps and early experiences.

M Mc K *Teacher*

****

Beatrice was incredible and can teach us all a few things about life being unfair, 100 years ago and now! I need to catch up on STEM, equality for women and what my kids must do towards their future! Love the extra detail in this more adult edition.

Freda D *Granny and lover of local history*

****

My girls are extremely interested in famous women, gender issues and equality for all, especially in the world of STEM: they all scratch an itch or two. They are blessed that their school leads the way in ensuring all pupils have a sound grounding in those subjects as well as the expected curriculum.

Beatrice Shilling's fame was unknown to us. My parents were unaware of her, too, so the book has educated the whole family. Having read the Tweens and Teens edition I looked forward to this edition which is more in depth, but does have some overlaps. That is to be expected.

Riding motorbikes and racing cars, fiddling with the engines and saving our pilots in WW2 was surprising to us all with the earlier edition, but the technical details and more about George were informative. Beatrice's early family history was interesting, too. Well done, B!

JW *Mother of four and Midwife*

****

A great book for STEM fans, those who love strong women in history and 'girls with grit'. The males in our world should enjoy it as well.

HGM *Grandad and amateur local historian*

****

To those who read, reviewed, offered advice and provided detailed
comments about the books, thank you so much.
You are amazing!

Elsie O'Neill
B.Ed (Hons) MSc.

DEDICATION

To My Family – you mean so much to me at all times.
Thank you for your support across both books and especially my husband's proof reading skills along with suggestions.

To Dennis Lock & David Woodford.
It is very much appreciated that both of you have given so much of your time, knowledge, photographs and permissions to help me get to know Beatrice in such depth.

I could never have written or published these books on Beatrice and her family without you both!

I treasure all your help and advice.

Much love to you all.
Grandma Elsie
xxxxxxx

CONTENTS

Baby Beatrice Basics

Beatrice (B) was born on Monday, March 8, 1909 at 4 Sidney Villas, London Road, Waterlooville, in Hampshire. It was the 67th day of the year and a day that would go down in history a century later. Beatrice was Annie Shilling's third child, Nora Alice being four at that time and Gladys Nancie three. Mum, Annie, called Nancy by friends and family reputedly came from a semi-famous family way back in time. Her maiden name was Dulake, possibly Du Lac anglicised.

The Shillings girls and Mum – Beatrice on her lap with one bare foot!
I have to be different even as a baby!
©David Woodford

Allegedly, her heritage can be traced back to **Sir Lancelot du Lac** (Lancelot of the Lake in French), supposedly one of King Arthur's Knights of the Round Table and possibly of Irish, Welsh or even German descent. *It sounds French to me, so let's go with that!*

WOW! Fact or fiction? Who knows?

Beatrice's Dad, Henry, who was fifty-two when he married Annie, was considered an old dad. He was previously a farmer before becoming a master butcher. Henry owned and employed staff in his fishmongers, butchers and game shops at the time when Waterlooville

was a just a small rural village and thought of as only a backwater *over the hill*' from nearby Portsmouth.

Waterlooville 1906
©Francis Frith

Today, Eric Jacksons, an electrical installation company, first established in 1928 is run by the third generation of Jacksons at 4 Sidney Villas. It is currently the oldest business surviving in Waterlooville and is still in the same premises as the Shillings' former enterprises.

Coincidentally, the Jacksons were operating their electrical business around the same time Beatrice had a few similar interests.

Jackson's electrical contractors and supplier premises at 4 Sidney Villas

Eric was a founder member of the Waterlooville Motorcycle Club, still in existence today, something worth recalling when you explore Beatrice's history later in this book.

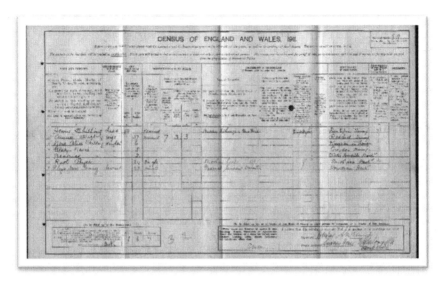

© Census 1911

The 1911 Census document detailed the names and occupations
of those living in the Shilling family household at that time. Henry,
aged 59, was listed as a *'Butcher, Fishmonger and Game* Dealer'*. He
was head of the household and employed two people:
Eliza aged 23 did domestic duties and Ruth aged 24 was a
'Mother's Help' with the children.
Their address was given as Sydney House Waterlooville.
His wife, Annie was 37 years of age, Nora was 6, Gladys 5 and the
youngest, Beatrice 2.

**A Game Dealer would have sold deer (venison), duck, partridge, rabbit, hare, pheasant,
grouse, wild boar and squirrel. Game is usually any meat from a hunted animal rather than
that raised on a farm.*

The Shilling Family: A little history is only the beginning …

Let's step back a little further …

Elizabeth Eliza Flint marries Alfred John Dulake

Beatrice's family can be traced back to her maternal grandparents and possibly further from extensive family ancestry searches. Her grandmother, Elizabeth Eliza Flint was born in Redhill, Surrey on August 4th 1832. Elizabeth's husband, Alfred John, was thought to be born around 1834 in Hastings, Sussex.

It has been suggested that perhaps Dulake was an anglicised version of the French name Du Lac; possibly derived so from somebody who originally lived by a lake many centuries ago as mentioned earlier.

Beatrice's grandparents married at St. Paul's Church in Deptford, Kent on March 5th 1862 when Elizabeth was 29 and Alfred 28.

At that time Deptford was part of Kent although is now designated to be within the boundaries of South East London.

St. Paul's, a member of the Church of England and within the Southwark Diocese, still stands today, although it suffered a fire a few years ago resulting in the loss of many stained glass windows. The church is Grade 1 listed and offers Mass in the Anglo-Catholic tradition.

It was considered to be one of London's finest 18th century English Italianate Baroque parish churches having been designed by Thomas Archer and built between 1712 and 1730 of Portland stone. Places of worship of this character and time in history are sometimes known as Queen Anne churches.

St. Paul's has been, *'dramatically preserved and recently restored in its spacious and peaceful churchyard.'*

www.achurchnearyou.com/church/621/about-us/

Alfred's address in the 1899 Kelly's Directory for Berkshire, Buckingham and Oxford was Castle Hill Lodge, St. Mark's Road, Berkshire. At other times it was St John's Terrace Road, Earlswood, Surrey as shown in the 1891 Census below.

Elizabeth and Alfred appear to have settled in Redhill with their seven children:

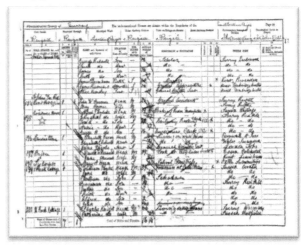

Emily born in 1863

Alfred John born in 1865

Ada L born in 1867

Harry Don Low born in 1869

Thomas Lanaway born in 1871

Annie Nancy born in 1873 – Beatrice's mum – and finally,

George H. born in 1875.

By the time Alfred senior was 47 and Elizabeth 49 in 1881, they had moved to Reigate in Surrey, a town which adjoins Redhill.

Both lived in that area at 16 St. John's Terrace Road until death; Alfred at 69 passing away in October 1901 and Elizabeth fourteen years later aged 83. Again in October, but in 1915, three months after the start of World War I.

Alfred had been a baking powder manufacturer, commission agent and grocer.

Beatrice's mother, Annie, known as Nancy, continued to live in Reigate until her marriage to Henry Shilling on April 16th 1904. Sadly her father had died before this. Annie Nancy was 30 and Henry was considerably older at 51. He had been a bachelor concentrating on his businesses and developing his skills as a Master Butcher just as his father Henry had, as evidenced on their marriage certificate.

Henry senior was born in 1819 in Odiham Hampshire and married Ann around 1848, then Mary in 1868. Beatrice's great-grandfather, John Shilling, was born in Odiham in 1781 and worked as a nurseryman. His wife was named Elizabeth and born in 1786.

Beatrice's parents, Henry and Annie Nancy were married in St. John's the Evangelist Church, Redhill. Similar to Annie's parents' church, St. John's is Anglican and part of the Church of England: it also belongs to the Southwark Diocese.

A year later, Annie Nancy gave birth to their first child Nora Alice on February 10th 1905 in Kingston on Thames.

NORA's Family

Nora, while at school was a studious character as were her sisters. They excelled at sports but found different careers when older. In 1920 the family moved again. This time to Dorking and the girls changed school to Dorking High School, Nora still preferring the domestic side of lessons at school, but excelling academically, too. Her needlework was first class.

At 21, Nora married Albert Edgar Woodford, a bank clerk, at St. Pauls Church in Dorking on July 18th 1926. He was eight and a half years older than Nora. The rank or professions of their fathers, Henry

and Frank, were both given as Gentlemen. Henry Shilling, Frank and Sarah Emily Woodford signed the register as all being present at the wedding.

Albert and Nora's first home appears to be 6 Norfolk Road, Dorking during 1929/30, possibly a rented house.

By 1932 they had moved to 23 West Hill Avenue Epsom, but not content in remaining there, by 1933 Nora and Albert were residing at 5 Upper Manor Road, Godalming, Surrey, perhaps due to moving up the property ladder or Albert's banking career. Nevertheless a further move came soon afterwards.

David advised,

"My father was promoted and transferred to the Godalming branch of Westminster Bank. After renting he purchased a new build - 7 Park Road, Godalming."

During 1935 it would appear from polling and other records that another upheaval took them to Hampton, Park Road, Godalming. However, this was not the case as David explained,

"Hampton is or was the name given to No 7. I have no idea who thought it up or where it came from. I do remember the houses being given numbers and starting at No 3! No 1 or 2! When Father bought a used car, a 1928 Triumph TR 1 for £30 (I have the bill) the gates rotted away but I do remember the wooden nameplate."

During 1951 Albert, Nora and a new addition to the family, Janet, still resided in Park Road, with an A. Shilling there, too! David recalled,

"First it shows A Shilling lived at No 7 - the same as us! And she did, she was Grandma! Mother's mother spent days with us or Aunt Beatrice at 'Carfield'. She was staying with Aunt Beatrice when she had a heart attack and died."

1959 saw Albert and Nora remaining there, having added another girl, Marian, to their family. A lovely sister for the delightful Janet and now Beatrice could boast about her second niece. She loved spending time with them when work permitted.

Over the years they gave Beatrice a nephew, David, another welcome addition to their family. He was born on March 5th 1932.

Now 89, David is mentioned in the book as his advice, knowledge, anecdotes and resources were essential in writing it. *He is an inspiring and knowledgeable e-mail mate.*

Sadly, Nora passed away aged 89 on October 11th 1994 while living at 7 Park Road, where they had lived since 1934. Take another look at David's photograph of the three girls with their mum – she was a beautiful looking child and no doubt quite stunning when older.

GLADYS

Annie Nancy and Henry added to their family on March 30th 1906 with Gladys Nancie. She preferred to be called Anne. Beatrice followed in 1909.

While the Shilling family was living at 58 Broughton Road, Thornton Heath in Surrey, Gladys was baptised at St. Saviours in Croydon on Thursday June 7th 1906.

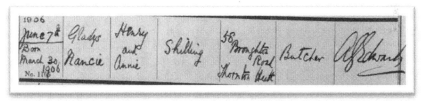

1937 documents showed Gladys, along with Beatrice and mum, Annie, living at Heatherbank, Burnt Hill Road, Frensham, Surrey. Henry, her father, having died the year before, was not listed on the Bourne Ward polling record.

When the 1939 Register was compiled Gladys was tracked down to living in Chapel En Le Frith, part of Derbyshire. Her name was updated from Shilling to Purves. It was quite normal at that time to do so and was crossed through in red ink. Purves may well have been her stage name as a ballerina or stage assistant, although unlikely to have it added to an official document. *More later.*

By the summer of 1953, Gladys had married Dennis Lock in Harrow, Middlesex. Again, this book could not have been written without Dennis' support, so we will visit him in further chapters to discover some of the interesting things he recalls about Gladys Nancie (Anne), his late wife. *Beatrice is investigated in greater detail later.*

Beatrice Tilly Shilling racing her Lagonda

The National Registration Act of 1939

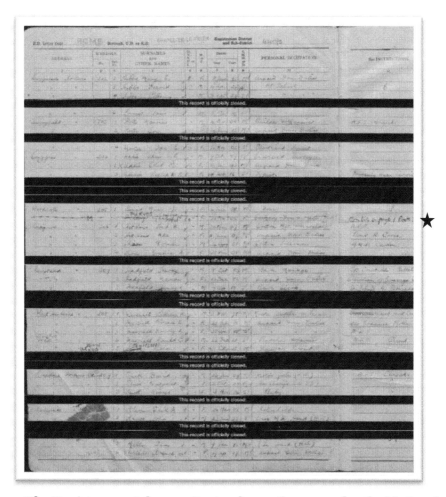

The Register was taken on September 29th 1939 under the National Registration Act of that year to take account of where people lived at that time for several reasons. It was also used to administer conscription for men between 18 and 41 years of age.

When Neville Chamberlain, the British Prime Minister at that time, declared war on Germany at 11.15 am on Sunday 3rd September

1939, Parliament immediately imposed The National Service (Armed Forces) Act compelling males of that age to register for military service.

The factual record was vital in issuing identity cards then later in January 1940, to provide ration books when goods were limited.

The Register provided details of where adults could be directed to work in each area as well as noting evacuations.

© *Alan & Margaret Martin's family; Stratford upon Avon*

Great Grandma's Identity Card

It was a civilian register as military personnel were not recorded, possibly for security at that time along with mass mobilisation. Military authorities recorded their own personnel based in army, RAF or naval establishments. However, if on leave, any military staff could be listed on the Register as well as civilians working in armed forces' bases. The Register comprised of the details of 40 million people across 65,000 transcript books.

Although not a census, it was set out along similar lines and included exact dates of birth whereas a census provided ages only. It only covered the populations in England and Wales. Other countries, such as Scotland and Northern Ireland held separate records.

The 1939 Register was based on plans which had been drawn up in preparation for the 1941 Census which never happened due to the war.

When the Register was released in 2015 a number of details were blanked out for privacy reasons; some people were still living and others had not reached 100 years of age. Access was via subscription only.

East London Building Home To 3 Children Hit By Bomb In The Year Of 1940
During The German Bombing Raids A.K.A. The Blitz
September 1940.
©New Times Paris Bureau Collection. (USIA)

Moving on: The Shilling Girls, and Dad, too!

Confusion arises when we anticipate the Shilling girls' names and who is who! Mum Annie, *known as Nancy*, was quite fortunate to have a domestic servant; 23 year old Eliza Jane Young came from Horndean, a few miles north of Waterlooville. As well as Eliza, Annie (Nancy) also had a mother's help/nanny in 24 year old Ruth Pryer from Southsea.

Southsea is approximately 12 miles away via the old London Road that literally ran from Portsmouth to London and back. It was a famous Victorian seaside resort with train connections to London. Queen Victoria regularly stopped off here on her way to Osborne House on the Isle of Wight (IOW).

Local streets are named after her family, too, e.g. Leopold St. Portsmouth itself was also a naval base with a famous dockyard. Today it berths cruise ships, cross channel and IOW ferries as well naval ships in the dockyard, including HMS Elizabeth, the navy's newest ship.

Southsea Seafront and Clarence Pier 1900s

For long distance travel, most people in the early 1900's used trains, but for shorter distances, horses and trams were more common. Ruth possibly took a train to Cosham from Southsea followed by a horse-drawn bus to Waterlooville. She may possibly have boarded the Horndean Light Railway tram as pictured here.

© JJMarshallsay 2020

In 1906 the cost was 1d (one old penny) from Cosham to the top of the hill where it terminated at the George Pub in Cosham, or 2d from there to Purbrook, near Waterlooville. For 5d (2p approximately today) she could go all the way to the terminus at Horndean, Eliza's village, but this was a little further than Waterlooville.

Ruth was responsible for the three children, so it appears the Shilling family were quite well off and fairly middle class.

The family moved around quite a lot but mostly between Surrey and Hampshire. Annie (Nancy) was born in Redhill Surrey while Dad, Henry, in Surbiton. *(Census 1911)* In 1914 they had returned to Surbiton.

Their first daughter, Nora Alice had been delivered in Kingston on Thames, while Gladys Nancie, known as Anne, was born in Croydon and Beatrice, always called Baby or B, in Waterlooville. As an adult she was also nicknamed Tilly. Find out why later.

Can you get your head around it? It may take some time, to sort out who was who!

Can you imagine doing all that moving around without a car and a removal company or van to shift your belongings? However, on reflection, even though the Shillings were well off, they would not have had the possessions we do in 2021. The technology in those days was very basic – television had been invented but was not freely available. The Shillings owned bicycles – important possessions for children if parents could afford them.

Showering daily, nocturnal hair washes and changing clothes on a daily basis are a must in most households today, but it would have been very different in the early 1900s. Baths would have been taken once a

week, if available, and shared with other siblings. The same clothes would usually be worn every day even when Spanish 'flu hit in 1918.

Beatrice aged four © Dennis Lock

A middle-class Edwardian lifestyle and education was the norm for the Shilling family and some others living at that time. Henry owed four shops in Surrey and he had the monopoly on selling meat etc. as his was the only butcher's establishment at that stage. Money was not short. Nothing changed much from this comfortable way of life that the Shillings enjoyed until the First World War affected the whole country. In January 1916 conscription was introduced for single men aged 19 to 41 when the Military Service Act was passed. Voluntary enlistment did not provide sufficient numbers of recruits without conscription.

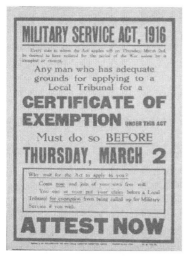

This did not apply to Beatrice's dad, Henry. He was much older at 63 and married.

A later Act in May that year, lowered the age to 18 and included married men, but retained the upper age at 41. ©*Wikipedia 2021*

Exemptions also applied to teachers, clergymen, doctors and those who were medically unfit as well as certain classes of industrial workers such as coal miners and those working in the iron and steel industries. These Scheduled or Reserved occupations were vital in keeping the country running. The men who produced ammunition and war equipment were considered essential to the whole war effort. © https://en.wikipedia.org

A tribunal was set up to investigate the circumstances of anyone who felt they should be excluded from a mandatory call-up. For example, those unfit due to poor health or disability,

family reasons such as hardship or being a conscientious objector.

Business owners could also apply with the aim of proving their business would suffer if conscripted.

Those who were exempted from military service were issued with badges and paperwork to prove they were carrying out *'war work'* at home as there was much opposition from local families when their men were sent off to war and others remained safely at home.

It would appear that Henry Shilling was exempted on many accounts which would have been a great relief to him and his family.

© *Pinterest military medical examinations*

Although the minimum age was 18 a number of young lads joined up to serve in the army, either through falsifying their dates of birth or just *'chancing their arm'*. At some point during or after the war the youngest British soldier was said to be a 12 year old fighting in France during 1917. He, along with others from different regiments, were sent back to Blighty.

A bit more on Gladys Nancie (Anne)

Research shows that Anne's surname Purves appears to have been from an earlier marriage to Charles Eric Purves, a Clerk in Holy Orders, which took place at the Parish Church in Barnstable, Devon on September 10th 1941. Charles lived at 10 Paiges Lane while Anne's address was given as 51 Landsdowne Crescent, Leamington Spa. He was 42 and Anne (Gladys) 35. Although known as a dancer, she gave her occupation as an engineer. Purves may well have been used as a stage name, too, but no evidence of that has been forthcoming.

David recalls his Aunt Anne.

"Yes Aunt Anne (Gladys) did marry Charles Purves who was connected to the church in some way. In my early teens I was sent by train to stay with them for a few days in Nottingham. He told me he 'saved people'... Eventually he gave that up and went on a Governmental Scheme to give employment to people in Oban making cement. My Mother and I drove there in my van and visited them."

Incidentally, Gladys hated her name and according to her second husband, Dennis Lock, never forgave her parents for their choice. However, she was always called Anne, her mother's real name, and responded to that rather than Gladys.

Dennis, who was 23 years younger than Anne, married her in 1953 without any disagreement from the Shilling family.

Henry was rather old at fifty-two when he married her mother, Anne, so would have been about 100 had he still been around in 1953. Recently Dennis recalled,

"(Gladys) Anne, whom I married in 1953 when we were 23 years apart in age, had always said she never forgave her parents for calling her Gladys. Everyone called her Anne. She signed official letters as Nancie. Anne died aged 103 in 2009. Anne had a full and interesting life, ballet trained and at one time stage assistant to famous illusionist Jasper Maskquelyn. Anne later obtained a London bachelor's degree in botany and chemistry."

Something to note for film buffs:

Benedict Cumberbatch is to play Jasper in a WWII drama based on David Fisher's book, The War Magician, who allegedly used his illusion skills to mislead Erwin Rommel in WWII.

"Born to a family of accomplished illusionists, Maskelyne worked as a stage musician in the 1930s before joining the British Army when World War II broke out. Together with a team of fellow illusionists whom he branded "the Magic Gang," Maskelyne claimed to have used his skills to make tanks, troops, and even buildings seem to disappear — playing what he said was a key role in the Allied effort to defeat the Nazis. However, some historians have argued that Maskelyne's part in the war effort was rather less vital than the illusionist himself claimed."

©www.bbcamerica.com/blogs/benedict-cumberbatchs-war-magician 2021

Will Anne's character appear in the drama as Jasper's assistant or will it just be his wife's role that gets a part?

Dennis also speaks highly of the Shilling family, especially his mother-in-law Nancy.

"Anne's mother (Nancy) was the sweetest, most generous lady and she supported our marriage (all our families did) in spite of the age difference. Henry ©https://en.wikipedia.org/ *Shilling, a crack shot at Bisley, (firing range) died before I met the family."*

Did Beatrice's initial interest in bikes stem from her Mum, Nancy? The photo portrays her as an elegant looking Edwardian lady.

Beatrice's Mum, Nancy on her bike around 1900 © Dennis Lock

Was it was difficult to ride her bike with such a beautiful long flowing dress?

The Shilling family returned to Surrey in 1914 when Beatrice was five and eventually she went on to Surbiton High School with her sisters where Beatrice was still known as B on entering the kindergarten.

Dennis mentioned that,

"Everyone in the close family called Beatrice simply 'B', which is how she signed family letters."

By all accounts, Beatrice wasn't an easy child. She was strong-willed, threw temper-tantrums, sometimes resulting in convulsions, and was known to bite her sisters, yet on most occasions they could play amiably. Beatrice would not retract her actions and apologise. *Sorry* wasn't a favourite word in use by Beatrice when she upset others either as a child or adult.

By 1920 the girls attended a grammar school in Dorking, where evidence of B's determination, temper and short fuse was demonstrated daily to the staff. In a letter to her husband, George, Beatrice confirms that her behaviour at school did not match her achievements in quality, while he appeared a more pleasant pupil.

"I don't think you were naughty enough at school – I was ticked off many times a day at school. I used to look so miserable that they used to apologise for talking so harshly. If you could establish that if you got ticked off you burst into tears you could get away with anything." (in Freudenberg 2003)

The Shilling girls would have been expected to attend church in those days. After all they were baptised and it was usual for families to send their children to Sunday school or all attend church. If so, it doesn't sound as though it improved B's attitude and behaviour.

Long ago, the church congregation and ministers often put the fear of God's wrath in children, so they generally did behave. *Some older adults recall it with horror.*

All three Shilling girls achieved highly, not only academically but also in domestic subjects such as needlework and sporting activities. While Nora happily produced household items such as tray cloths, the other two girls much preferred to tinker around with tools and make artefacts from natural materials such as wood. Nora, in later life, also married and, according to her brother-in-law Dennis,

"Had three children, David, Janet and Marian. Nora was tall (unlike her sisters) but when she died had shrivelled pathetically owing to osteoporosis. She was a talented amateur artist and a very efficient mother and housewife."

David, Nora's son, recalls Beatrice with fondness.

"We loved our Aunt B. She was very close to my mother and my sisters and I benefitted."

Beatrice aged 20
©Manchester University

Tinkering times

Beatrice enjoyed tinkering with Meccano, although her construction kit of perforated strips and angled brackets etc. were made from sheet metal or perhaps tin plated, while currently, 100 years later, it is mostly plastic. The older bits from the 1950s and before is much more solid than the newer plastic kits and sells for a fortune on e-bay and at auctions.

Frank Hornby, manufacturer of the famous trains invented Meccano around 1900. He ran competitions for model makers and also sold Meccano magazines for one (imperial) penny. Did Beatrice ever compete with her models in that boys' world? *Indeed she did.* Apparently, Beatrice became so proficient with her Meccano construction kits that at twelve she entered, and won a prize in a national competition set by Meccano Magazine. Verity, from Waterlooville Library explained that:

"Beatrice's entry was a working model of a spinning wheel, inspired by seeing one in use at an exhibition she visited with her mother."

Meccano 1911/2 © www.alansmeccano.org

Roger Marriott very kindly found an article in one of his treasured collections of Meccano Magazines (MM) from 1921/2.

"I have only been able to find one reference to Beatrice Shilling in the MM. She gained an "additional prize" in the 1920/21 competition begun in 1920 and published in the MM July-August 1921.

She is listed as 'Beatrice Shilling, 65a South Street, Dorking, Surrey; Spinning Wheel' in the section for competitors aged between 10 to 14 years of age.

There is no picture of the model and I cannot find any further mention of her."

© *www.nzmeccano.com*

Having established an exact date an internet search revealed electronic copies of old Meccano Magazines including the July – August 1921/2 one in which Beatrice was mentioned. It is not very clear, hence the stars to identify her, but more proof of her win and skills at only twelve. *David, her nephew was thrilled to have a copy.*

It was a delight to hear this from Roger as she may have been excluded from any write-up being female, or if in fact, it was a local dealer's competition she had participated in. Roger also mentioned a local event at that time; surprisingly a Meccano Club for girls!

"There is a note in Sept/Oct 1921 of a club in Claygate, Surrey of the formation of a girl's club to complement a boy's also running at this time but it does not seem to be close to Dorking, and there is no mention of members."

Thank you, Roger, for tracking down this information.

Are there any Meccano clubs locally running today and if they are female only? Apparently, the clubs are worldwide as far afield as Australia and Argentina!

Beatrice was **ambidextrous**, as David her nephew explained.

"Beatrice would change hands with her pencil when going from the right to left side of a piece of paper."

Try it. Aim to produce an accurately formed image using both hands. However, it must have been so useful later in life when dexterity, speed and skill mattered most to B.

During an interview with Woman Engineer magazine Beatrice recalled her childhood.

It seems she enjoyed mechanical engineering even then.

"As a child I played with Meccano, I spent my pocket money on penknives, an adjustable spanner, a glue pot and other simple hand tools."

©www.bbc.co.uk/news/uk-england-manchester-40267364

Quite unusual for a female 100 hundred years ago, unlike the 21st century when children are given more equal opportunities.

Most primary and secondary schools aim to instil a love of science and maths, as well as other *__STEM__ subjects in school and to take that learning and experience home to further develop skills and understanding.

__Computing at Schools__ (CAS) is an excellent way to pass on skills and new ideas for teachers and parents to further develop skills with children and each other.

https://www.computingatschool.org.uk/

So much is on the internet for free to support it for all ages. Try Scratch for yourself or Daisy the Dinosaur with young children. Lego enthusiasts will love LEGOWEDO2

https://scratch.mit.edu/

With Scratch, you can program your own interactive stories, games, and animations — and share your creations with others in the online community.

Scratch helps young people learn to think creatively, reason systematically, and work collaboratively — essential skills for life in the 21st century.

Scratch is designed, developed, and moderated by the Scratch Foundation, a non-profit organization. It is provided free of charge.

*__STEM__ *– science, technology, engineering and maths – please see glossary for more detailed information; also STEAM. Check out the* __Stemettes__*, too.*

Beatrice – the teenage years

At school in Dorking, engineering and things of a mechanical nature were certainly classed as *'boys' toys'* in that era, but Beatrice did not let that stop her. *A dilemma? No, she did what she wanted! She had determination.*

There is no doubt Beatrice was a very intelligent young lady, although lady-like is probably not a word used to describe her. She spoke her mind and did as she pleased; was a bit of a tom-boy and not always very feminine in her dress sense or activities. By all accounts Beatrice was not very polite or well-mannered at times.

Royal Enfield ©Richard Red Devil Motors

By fourteen Beatrice, with additional finance from Anne, had purchased a second-hand motorbike; a two-stroke Royal Enfield on which she competed against her two sisters riding their pedal cycles. Anne occasionally rode pillion behind Beatrice.

Beatrice became adept at taking it apart and improving the reliability of the engine. Whilst doing so, she developed skills and knowledge about its mechanics and intricacies, possibly far beyond that of many lads of her age. All that fiddling around with Meccano, spanners and a penknife proved invaluable while tinkering about with her bikes to advance their performance. *Beatrice had several bikes in her lifetime and continued to defy conventions.*

Stripping and reassembling the rifles belonging to her father, Henry, was another of Beatrice's pastimes. According to Dennis, B's brother-in-law, Henry had been an expert shot as a young man, winning prizes in a variety of events. By all accounts, he was a skilled marksman. *Beatrice would follow in his steps later in life.*

Bisley in Surrey, where Henry honed his gun skills, has been the base of the National Rifle Association since 1890, but nowadays is also a Site of Special Scientific Interest (SSSI) due to a wide range of fauna and flora, so cannot be developed for building work.

Henry had joined the Twelfth Surrey Rifle Volunteer Battalion long before his marriage to Annie. Although Henry was too old for active service in 1914, the century prior to this saw many such divisions established in order to train men ready for war should the need arise. Training consisted of drills, marching, yearly camps and rifle shooting contests; all good practice should military intervention or call-up be required.

He excelled in competitions, winning the Queen's Prize for his Battalion in 1877. Beatrice proudly displayed and used his prize, a mantelpiece clock, in her home over a century later. Making his own ammunition may have been one of his other skills bearing in mind the advice he gave Beatrice when teaching her how to handle a gun. Henry also taught his wife, Annie, in case of attack when WWI commenced. It was also known as the Great War, due to the enormous scale of the conflict at that time compared to previous battles.

Beatrice's technical skills as a writer stood her in good stead when she explained about Henry's love of guns and expertise to the readers of Guns Review in 1978.

"At the outbreak of the Great war, the Army asked for Service-type rifles and my father handed in several. However, in case of invasion, he kept two and a good supply of ammunition – he was a Reservist and mother had shown some promise with a Lee-Metford. His rifles and ammunition were never locked up, but safety rules on handling were strictly enforced – which made the rifles rather unrealistic 'props' for 'Cowboys and Indians' and other war games! Being interested I learned how a rifle worked, how to clean it, and how important cleaning was.

When I was older I was taught how to fire a 303 and this was done quite informally, firing into the chalk of the Surrey Hills. The advice I remember was,

"Take each shot separately. Don't hurry – the last shot is as important as the first. Always fire experimental rounds remotely and not in a gun you value."

Later in life, Beatrice was also a crack shot but at Camberley Pistol Club and very competitive in many ways: her favourite tasks and sports generally thought of as being suitable for only the male species at that time.

Some girls today believe that weak males are intimidated by and show anxiety in the company of strong females. Beatrice, as an extremely intelligent and strong woman would have felt the same and by all accounts showed it, too. *She would take no prisoners.* Her uncanny ability to do as she pleased and tell others what she thought, even if rudely done, was often evident. She could be fierce, aggressive, outspoken and relentless in pursuit of her goal. **Let's call it determination!**

Other strong women at that juncture in time would have done the same and increasingly, women are standing up for their rights today, too.

Motor biking and racing were approached with the same attitude and determination.

Beatrice would not have had to meet all the current regulations there are today prior to riding a motor cycle. There would have been plenty of country lanes or fields to compete with Nora's and Anne's bikes in and around the Surrey countryside. The Roaring Twenties appears quite an apt name, though not linked to Beatrice's and her acquaintances' love of speed during the 1920s.

Beatrice riding her Matchless V/2, a 1928 Sports Model while at Manchester University (1929 – 1932). ©Dennis Lock)

A motivating female biker

Alfonsina Strada, an Italian cyclist may well have inspired Beatrice in her endeavours to race bikes. Another motivating, tom-boy, biking female, who sadly died in 1959 of a heart attack as she returned home after watching a bike race. *What a way to go; filled with the adrenaline and joy of racing.* She was one of only thirty cyclists to finish a 21 day race around steep Italian mountains even though 90 started off together.

The following year, she was banned from racing as officials declared the Giro d'Italia was for men only. *REALLY!* It is quite unjust just how prejudiced this whole gender issue was and still is today, although improving somewhat. Similar to Beatrice, she rode push bikes and motorcycles. Beatrice must have been aware of Alfonsina who was nicknamed, *'the devil in a dress'.* Whereas B would have worn men's trousers!

However, her sheer determination did not make her hesitate one bit. She raced and held the speed record for 26 years!

Alfonsina 1924
©podiumcafe.com

Remember, like Strada, Beatrice's middle name was determination!

Women's intellect and skills are not inferior to men's!

By the time she was fifteen in 1924, Beatrice had firmly decided that her future lay ahead in engineering and sought an appropriate apprenticeship on leaving school in 1926. They were not readily open to females.

Her expertise in what is now called STEM subjects paved the way for her future. She was great at maths and science, never mind the skills she attained with mechanics and engineering through stripping and rebuilding her motorbike. In addition she understood the importance of cleaning guns accompanied by the whys and wherefores of their assembly and usage along with important safety procedures.

Beatrice had an excellent brain and again, determination to succeed in her chosen sphere. Not only did she need that challenge in life but she desperately needed to enjoy what she was doing. Frustration, anger and deep dissatisfaction was promised in practically any other field of work, not helped by the lack of appropriate career support from school.

At that time, women in engineering was almost unheard of. Unemployment was high, often exceeding one million at any given time. Men feared that women could *'steal'* their chances of employment from them, often on lower wages, but not through lack of skill. Female competition was frowned upon. Women were still very much considered second class citizens; fit only for marrying, having children, looking after their homes and pandering to their men.

Beatrice's stars must have been in the correct alignment as Dorking High School received a letter, sent to many schools, from the Association of Headmistresses in Public Secondary Schools. It was jointly sent with the Ministry of Labour and the Department of Employment and Insurance advising of a scheme conceived by two leading female stalwarts in engineering.

During 1919, seven pioneering females came together to set up the **Women's Engineering Society** (WEA). It was set up to help protect the rights of female workers who had been employed during WWI in various aspects of the engineering industry. Many of these women had manufactured arms and ammunition for the war effort while their men were on the front line. A high number enjoyed their work and wished to continue but were expected to relinquish their employed once the men were home; including those that had been widowed during the war and needed the income and camaraderie of the workplace.

Training and opportunities in engineering were high on their agenda, something which is still well established in 2021. Although in the early days there were disagreements about it being a purely professional body but the education and 'work experience' type openings won the day.

Laura Wilson, Caroline Haslett & Margaret Partridge © IET

During the 1920s the Electricity Supply Acts (1919 and 1922), Acts to amend the Law to supply electricity, failed to do as planned. The latter Act permitted financial borrowing to undertake the schemes, but only four joint electricity authorities had been created. Different currents and frequencies deemed the supply of electricity a failure at that time. Standardisation of frequency was a specific requirement, so it was superseded in 1926 by a new Act which gave electricity commissioners the power to establish a Central Electricity Board (ECB) and the formation of the National Grid, mainly completed by 1935. The commissioners could control the Grid, but did not own the power stations set up to supply the electricity.

Margaret Partridge B.Sc and Caroline Haslett, Director of the Electrical Association for Women, who were resilient members of the Women's Engineering Society, were those strong stalwarts responsible for circulating the letter to schools during May 1926. Margaret seized the opportunity to expand her electricity company and benefitted greatly with the new Act coming into force later that year when it received Royal Assent on December 15th 1926.

An electrical engineer with vision, Margaret, along with Caroline the WEA's secretary, were to change Beatrice's life forever with a move to Bungay, in Suffolk for initial training prior to work elsewhere. Margaret provided Beatrice with this opportunity in her electrical engineering company. The letter to schools read,

"An exceptionally interesting vacancy has been notified to the committee. Miss Partridge BSC, director of the Exe Valley Electricity Co., and other Electrical undertakings in Devonshire is at present engaged in a contract for the generation and installation of electricity

at Bungay, Suffolk, and requires a pupil to learn the work at Bungay.

The training will aim at making the selected girl proficient to assist in taking charge of the plant and electrical development of the district." (in Freudenberg 2003)

Annie Shilling encouraged B to apply once the academic year was drawing to a close that summer. She knew Beatrice had the maths and physics along with preferring physical and hands-on work to stand a good chance of being considered for the apprenticeship. Henry, her father, was not encouraging, but neither did he oppose it.

Margaret had ambitious plans to open up three or four power stations each year in the west of England, with Caroline recruiting new apprentices to be trained. In turn they would then train the next novice. By the end of their training in 2 – 3 years' time, it was expected that each student would become a fully-fledged electrical engineer capable of running each power station unaided.

She was becoming impatient for apprentice applications and only a month later wrote to Caroline wondering if she had made an error of judgement in requesting females to apply rather than a male. Matthew Freudenberg (2003) quoted part of her letter,

"Re this damsel – do you really think there is any likelihood of a girl presenting herself who wants to learn engineering? ...

If I had ever thought that it would take so long I wouldn't have troubled about the engineering side – but just taken on a typist and started with a boy or young man for the engineering side."

Perhaps nobody else had applied. However, Beatrice was employed by Margaret for three years installing wiring and generators as electricity was brought to homes and businesses in the out-lying

River Exe Valley. Beatrice was installed in Bampton, just south of Exmouth, Margaret having sorted accommodation for her at the local Young Women's Christian Association (YWCA) hostel.

Margaret wearing her fur coat to the left of Beatrice
© *https://ietarchivesblog.org/*

Working with Dr John Archibald Purves, an eminently distinguished electrical graduate from Edinburgh University, Margaret's enterprising skills and sheer determination ensured additional sites were contracted, too. This provided the 17 year old Beatrice, who, incidentally, should have been 18 for the *'apprenticeship'* in hand, with additional experience.

One of Margaret's lists of 'DON'Ts' to her apprentices and engineers working in the engine room included:

> *"Don't use a hammer or heavy tool to hit engines with*
> *Don't loosen nuts and bolts on an engine and forget to tighten*
> *them again and*
> *Don't touch a spark plug when the engine is running."*
> IET Archives 12.12.19.

As mentioned earlier, Beatrice was not lady-like at all. Matthew Freudenberg, in Beatrice's biography references Margaret Partridge's letter to her friend Caroline Haslett, Secretary of the WEA.

> *"I have managed to give Beatrice Shilling over a week's wiring*

work, and it seems to be turning out a great success. I really think she is a great acquisition to the firm – able to enjoy any new experience – and not in the least superior or blasé – the fault of the very young at times. She has a wicked joy in making all the YWCA hostel stand their hair on end by tales of her unladylike exploits when wiring."

For this, Beatrice earned twenty five shillings a week – in decimal terms the equivalent of £1.25, which would appear to be worth considerably more today, but due to inflation £1 today does not buy as much as it did in 1927. Apprentices in Beatrice's time were lower paid in monetary terms (actual coins or notes) in relation to today. Nowadays apprentices rely more on technology and so expect to be paid better as the cost of living is high, too.

As time went by, Margaret was more than aware of Beatrice's potential. Her friend, a Miss Rowbothom, who joined the South West Electricity Company (SWEC) as a partner in 1927, taught Beatrice advanced maths as she, too, knew what B was capable of doing. Even though Beatrice was deemed only an external linesman in addition to her electrical wiring installations internally in buildings and homes, plans were afoot to teach her design and generating plant lay out projections. She succeeded highly here and advanced her skills tremendously. Following on from this Margaret believed she would make an extremely proficient engineer. She knew Beatrice needed more than what the SWEC could offer her, so persuaded her to apply to Victoria University in Manchester for a place to study electrical engineering. Should B give up working and a wage or struggle financially at university? A better education may provide an improved income in a more interesting situation later on. A dilemma and one still faced by students and others today.

Beatrice was one of only two females to undertake this pioneering course commencing in October 1929 and had to borrow the £1000 needed for her fees. The National Society for Women's Services provided it free of interest, possibly via Margaret's influence and knowledge of Beatrice. A local girl, Sheila McGuffie, was the other innovative female student, who like Beatrice did not find it easy competing in a man's world.

Beatrice and Sheila at Victoria College Manchester © Manchester University

Another friend, Eileen Shephard, who preferred to be called Muriel (later Breed), whom Beatrice met while working at Ferranti during an eight week holiday job, matched B in her love of bikes and sense of humour. They shared a room in Muriel's parents' house, B teaching her maths and physics. This supplemented the girl's evening class tuition, helped her understand it better and pass her electrical diploma examination. The girls remained friends for life, both retaining their ironic sense of humour and a love of motorcycles even when married some years later. Fighting for women's rights was another joint enterprise, which enabled them to do what they wanted in a male orientated world.

Muriel

University lecturers encouraged students to participate in additional classes in linked subjects such as mechanical engineering, and thermaldynamics as well as electrical subjects, all of which they did.

It wasn't all work and no play for the girls, who had developed different interests. Although Sheila was sporty and played lacrosse and hockey they were not important to Beatrice who retained her love of bikes, so joined a motorcycle club enabling her to compete in trials in the nearby northern Derbyshire and Greater Manchester area of the Peak District.

Beatrice retained not only her love of motor biking, but also the tinkering skills she developed as a teenager improving her Royal Enfield. While at Manchester she invested in a Matchless Model V/2 which she used to ride in both sidecar and solo trials. The bike was considered to be the Super Sports model with a 495cc overhead valve engine. The sidecar could topple easily going around corners or if knocked carelessly. Sheila did ride in the sidecar at times but proved too light a weight to keep it positioned properly.

Incidentally during WWII Matchless produced 80,000 G3 and G3L bikes for the armed forces!

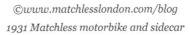

©*www.matchlesslondon.com/blog*
1931 Matchless motorbike and sidecar

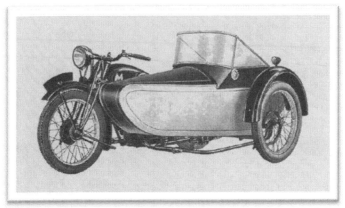

Matchless bikes - made for the police force

Beatrice also became a heavy smoker, something that added to her outgoings, but it has been suggested that her parents topped up her income to cover the bikes etc. as her loan was solely for University fees.

Beatrice's first degree wasn't enough for her, so after graduating in 1932 with a 2nd Class honours, she continued her education by completing a Master of Science degree in Mechanical Engineering.

Her chosen area of study was to research the working temperatures of pistons across two-stroke diesel engines of various kinds. Unusually at that time for a female, her outstanding ability ensured that she received a grant from the Department of Engineering. Government grants had been cut back due to high unemployment and reduced spending across all sections for both male and female applicants.

At that stage job opportunities were extremely limited, more so for a female in engineering, as it was still thought of as employment for men. *How dare a woman even contemplate doing skilled men's work regardless of aptitude and ability!*

© *Dennis Lock (in Freudenberg 2003)*

Educated females were encouraged to become nurses and teachers, though not doctors or scientists, and certainly not engineers, positions reserved for the male species of this world at that point in history and for decades to follow.

For many years women were not allowed to vote either; their brains being thought of as rather fragile and incompetent to that of men and therefore unable to make such crucial choices as electing an MP. In 1917, women aged 30 and over were at last given the vote. Younger women were still not allowed to vote.

Yet during WWI, between 1914 and 1918, an estimated two million women replaced men in employment, proving that women were just as capable as their male counterparts. However, the Second World War was just around the corner and women were again needed to do men's work when they were shipped off to fight as before. For a second time the female workers were expected to give it up once the war ended and the men returned. They were paid less, too!

Something Beatrice was not too happy about when she was further employed in a vital occupation a few years later.

Were males' egos too delicate to compete equitably with women who were just as skilled, if not more so, than themselves? After all, many women work full-time, raise their children and still undertake the majority of household tasks, even today in this so called liberated world.

"There are those who say that bullying is behind all forms of violence, conflict, persecution, abuse, harassment, discrimination, and prejudice."

"All cruelty springs from weakness."—Seneca, 4BC-AD65

©*www.goodtherapy.org*

Only weak men are worried about competition from strong and dynamic women. Never let them bully you!

By the way, even Henry, Beatrice's father, was not too enamoured with her chosen profession until she successfully wired a bedroom light with a two-way switch to enable him to have a control by the bed as well as next to the door!

Her mother supported her, though. All the way!

Pioneering women scientists and mathematicians who changed the world

Beatrice would surely have been aware of pioneering women scientists such as **Grace Hopper** born three years before her in the USA.

Grace Hopper Computer Scientist © Wikipedia

She tinkered with clocks as a child then went on to help the Navy decode enemy messages during WWII with her brilliant computing skills. Grace even became a Rear Admiral in the US navy!

Rear Admiral Grace Hopper © Wikipedia

Awe-inspiring mathematicians such as Ada Lovelace, who worked with **Charles Babbage** on the first computer, long before computers as we know them today were invented, may well have been familiar to Beatrice, too. The 'Difference Engine' computer actually ran on a steam engine and calculated quite complex algorithms as Ada enhanced it but in the language of that day. Algorithms are basically instructions; today children at primary school learn about them though coding or maths.

Interestingly enough, *Ada studied birds to determine the perfect balance between body weight and wing size, but alas did not manage to soar into the tropopause – up to 10k high in the sky - never mind the stratosphere, approximately 30k up. However, flying was something Beatrice did eventually achieve.

Every year, Ada is the topic of conversation to open an international celebration of the achievements

Ada Lovelace © Alfred Chalon
in Wikipedia

women make in STEM subjects: science, technology, engineering and maths. The plan is to highlight the importance of women working in STEM as well as encourage females to take up careers in that field. *Think about it girls!*

People meet and listen to others talk about their work and research, but in a very informal manner. In between, they blog, use Twitter, make **podcasts** and post on Facebook to promote gender equality in engineering, education and the local communities across the world.

Regardless, you can catch up on those wonderful women pushing the cutting edge of science to make a difference while changing the face of science, technology, engineering and maths. *Females need to do it!*

*You may be interested to know that every year on the second Tuesday in October, Ada is remembered by a special STEM day – The Ada Lovelace Day (ALD)!

Did Beatrice ever consider Formula One racing?

With her bike and later car racing expertise Beatrice may well have fancied being a Formula One driver like the Italian Lella Lombardie. During the Spanish Grand Prix in 1975, she finished sixth, the first female to do so in a World Champion race. These Italian women appear to be made of stern stuff and sheer determination in a man's world!

Lella Lombardi reading in the pit garage at Silverstone during a six hours race in 1976
© Wikipedia

Many women, and some men, believe that women's strength and ability should not be compromised, ignored or sneered at. Celebrate diversity and battle peacefully, but staunchly for gender equality.

Mahatma Gandhi believed that,

"Our ability to reach unity in diversity will be the beauty and the test of our civilisation."

Women must never give up.

Motorbikes and sidecars

Nevertheless, not to be deterred by male arrogance and discriminatory rules in the workplace, Beatrice decided to further her engineering experience by investigating the behaviour of super-charged cylinder engines while working with **Professor Graham Mucklow** as his research assistant. Fortunately, her skills and expertise were recognised along with forthcoming funding to undertake further study in his engineering department at Manchester University. He later worked in Birmingham.

© *www.gracesguide.co.uk/*

Beatrice was able to undertake research to support the professor, analysing any readings she recorded as well as constructing parts for test equipment. She also developed further skills in using brazing equipment and lathes, something which stood her in good stead when it came to her racing hobby. Beatrice used these skills to improve her motorcycle engines and in particular her newly acquired Norton 490cc at a cost of around £70, possibly with a trade-in reduction for her Matchless. Mum and Dad may well have helped. See B's image riding her Matchless bike on page 26 and a sidecar example on page 42.

Her experience here helped Beatrice transform her Norton into a much faster machine, though not without problems on the race track.

Beatrice never allowed accidents to stop her. Her thirst for speed was more important than broken bones!

Can you just imagine what Beatrice would be doing if still alive and of working age in today's society? The mind boggles at all the possibilities. Would she be beating the current Formula One drivers such as Lewis Hamilton in his Mercedes and Sebastian Vettel steering his Ferrari around a race track? Perhaps she'd have arrived in space, her later rocket knowledge being put to the test.

Beatrice never abandoned her hobbies or old motor bike, continuing to tinker with the engine to improve its performance. Not

only had she now got additional skills due to her engineering experience, but also a growing passion for motorcycles. During her time improving her education and throughout her early career, Beatrice began racing regularly on the famous Brooklands track in Surrey. Her bike trials days were over.

She made her dreams come true in a man's world. She was determined.

© *Brooklands Race Track Advert*

Brooklands was the world's first purpose built circuit especially for motor racing. Once again, Beatrice never flinched at embracing male competitors, this time on the racing track. She was a great exponent for women's liberation and a true '*suffragette*', taking on men's roles and exceeding their ability, too. Beatrice never believed a woman had an inferior mind or skills to the men around her.

Her early races at Brooklands began with a new members' event held in June 1934. As a fledgling member of the British Motor Cycle

47

Racing Club she achieved highly obtaining 6th place in her first race followed by 3rd in her second. She was new to the track having only completed a few practice laps. Being female she received some exceptional praise in write-ups, especially when she was prepared to race against the male experts of that time, some being renowned professional riders. An unusual accolade for females in the 1930s, but less so in present times.

In today's society we aspire to celebrating our differences, encouraging diversity but above all learning what we can. We teach our children to be kind and thoughtful and think before they speak. People across the world strive for this to eventually eradicate prejudice and unjust behaviour. However, Beatrice did not always think before she spoke, although not in a prejudiced manner. *It was more of a case that she didn't suffer fools gladly.* Beatrice had a well-known reputation for

speaking her mind, quite unkindly at times, too, as you will hear more about later.

Over time Beatrice had upgraded her bike to a **Norton Manx 500**. The bike was used to travel to work. However, during August 1934 with some engine fiddling and her interchangeable hands, the now very experienced Beatrice managed to be the fastest female on two wheels. Sadly, it could no longer provide a ride to work without reverting it back to its former glory as not permitted on the road with the changes needed to race at speed.

Beatrice achieved a speed exceeding 101 miles per hours (mph) while completing the 2.75 mile (4.43km) circuit in record time. B was awarded the prestige Gold Star for her performance: the envy of many males at that time and the fastest woman on two wheels, although Fanny Blenkiron was the first female to gain her Star during April 1934!

Motor Cycling, published by Temple Press, reported,

"A feature of the first handicap was the brilliant riding of Miss B. Shilling on a very standard-looking 490cc Norton. After a slowish first lap, she made up for lost time with a second circuit of 101.02 mph, thus joining the select ranks of Gold Star holders, being the second woman motorcycle racer to do so.'

A Yorkshire Post & Leeds Intelligence article *(27.08.1934)* entitled, **"GIRL RIDER'S FEAT" 101mph on a Motor-Cycle at Brooklands** is even more impressive. It tells how Beatrice achieved her Gold Star lapping the track at 101mph. She finished third.

"Her sensational descent at 'the home of speed' came at the end of her annual holiday."

The judges were so impressed with her results they handicapped her in the next race, allowing a male to have a head start of 17 minutes and 16 seconds thus winning the race at a speed much lower than B's, a mere 82.18 mph! She missed third place by a yard (0.9144m).

Although the handicapped races were meant to be fair, it reeks of gender issues and poor male egos again. *There is little doubt that the judges were men!*

Sadly, this situation was accepted by many at that time. Beatrice excelled and outraced many established professional male riders such as Noel Pope, born the same year as B, on his super-charged Brough Superior. Over time his bike became a legend while his ego was rather dented along with that of other males.

"From the 33 second mark Miss Shilling on her self-tuned Norton ran through the field, and with one Lap at 101.64 m.p.h. and one lap at 102.69 provided a somewhat unexpected win." (Motor Cycle July 1935)

Ben Bickell came second and Noel third, both of them highly professional bikers. Being defeated by a female was not something Noel Pope or other males expected, especially a novice biker.

© *www.inventricity.com/tilly-shilling Beatrice posing for a Norton advert*

The Portsmouth Evening News reported on this success at Brooklands *(Thursday 27th June 1935, page 7)*

"Miss Beatrice Shilling, a 25-year- old Master of Science, won a motor-cycle race at Brooklands at 97mph, from famous men riders"

Not only was Beatrice a female, but in addition, an extremely clever young lady who was winning to high acclaim in a male world.

Charles Mortimer, who raced cars and bikes at Brooklands during the 1930s, took the credit for teaching Beatrice to improve her racing style and skills in order to reach high speeds, however, it is possible that through determination she would have achieved similar results regardless of his intervention and expertise.

Following on from WWII, when racing recommenced, Charles and his wife raced cars at Silverstone and Goodwood, two tracks where Beatrice became quite familiar with in later life.

Charles Mortimer at Brooklands © Mat Oxley

Mat Oxley, the former motorcyclist and journalist tells the tale in his book *Speed (2018)*, of how Charles overheard a conversation about the upcoming races while astride one of the Brooklands' toilets.

At that time, to be fair to all riders with different machines, races were often handicaps rather than *'scratch'* competitions. The slowest bikes and new riders would get a head start over the competent experts with powerful machines handicapped to start last. The plan being that the riders would finish around the same time with cheers from the spectators. They usually caught up early on over a few laps and came in the first trawl to cross the line, so it didn't always work as the timekeepers had intended, but plans were hatched to change this.

Charles' eavesdropping enlightened him to race fixing. He learned that the races had already been decided by the top three bikers and the bookies would lose out while they personally gained financially. Over seven or eight races this could be quite lucrative for the motorcyclists. According to Charles, even the reporters fell for the scam and, along with the crowds watching, thought it was one of the best day's racing they were privileged to witness.

Hugh Fortescue Locke King was the British entrepreneur who founded and financed the racing circuit at Brooklands in 1906, it finally opening in 1907. He was determined to improve racing speeds for the English enthusiasts as the French could travel at much higher speeds than those in England.

At one stage, it was recorded that a French car reached an impressive speed of 108mph on a public road while here in the UK the speed limit was restricted to a maximum of 12mph.

Brooklands racing track was constructed of a concrete surface with two straight runs joined by two long semi-circular bends totalling three and a quarter miles in length. Importantly, it was considered a safe track at average speeds up to 120mph. However, during the twenty-eight years of racing it had many horrendous crashes and at least seventeen deaths. This included three spectators, two mechanics and the remainder being drivers.

Brooklands provided an exciting and competitive setting for both Beatrice and her future husband, George Naylor, to race their modified bikes, the latter often being entered for races by his wife. Beatrice was short and could not always reach the handlebars due to the seat being positioned too far to the rear after their numerous modifications. George, on the other hand, was much taller and therefore had the stretch to reach from behind the new fuel tank to the front of the

supercharged Norton with more ease. Beatrice had fitted an air-blower which fed into the petrol tank and acted as a compressed air reservoir.

World War II in September 1939 ended racing at Brooklands, but there would be other competitions and races at different venues once racing resumed after the war ended in 1945.

The Royal Aircraft Factory Farnborough

An impending war ensured the rearmament of Britain occurred to be prepared for any attack by the Germans, Italians or Japanese. Historically, the Royal Aircraft Factory, later the RAE, and other manufacturers had a well-established programme of research and development in aircraft manufacture. The RA Factory moved to the current site in 1905 having outgrown previous premises; initially the Balloon School in Woolwich, Chatham and Aldershot. On April 1st 1911, it was re-named His Majesty's Aircraft Factory and known as the Royal Aircraft Factory

Mervyn O'Gorman controlled the factory and did much to establish Farnborough as a centre of first class research while collaborating with the National Physical Laboratory based in Teddington, London. Mervyn's team were experts in all forms of aeronautics ensuring Farnborough was one of the most forward thinking research establishments in the world. Scientific results established via testing etc. were applied to full scale aircraft.

1914 saw the War Office agree to financing the research of engines as well as the design and construction of aircraft at Farnborough. In addition, the testing of armaments, instruments, airframes, electrical and wireless fittings were also undertaken by 5,000 adults of both genders by 1915. Test pilots, technical staff, and scientific officers were employed as well as administrators to keep the factory running well and meet with demand.

However, private manufacturers were increasingly growing

discontented as it appeared that the factory was consuming large amounts of funds from the War Office to build fighter planes and competition was unfair.

It was decided to cease building aircraft and instead develop techniques in scientific research to build wind tunnels, engines, structural equipment, instruments and metallurgy. This research and development resulted in improved knowledge of aerodynamics and structures hence allowing Britain to lead the way in powered flight.

When WWI ended in 1918, the factory was renamed once more to the RAE and limited finance ensured its work was rapidly scaled down along with staff numbers dropping to 1,000. Research and evolution in aerodynamics continued, but at a much reduced level, so that by the 1920s the funding declined, mainly due to economic pressures following the war. The war was over, so defence required less financial support.

On August 19th 1934, Adolf Hitler, already the chancellor of Germany since January 1933, was elected president of the republic, demonstrating an unprecedented consolidation of power. He increased his military presence over the next few years giving rise to possible threats of war which the British government took as a serious probability.

The threats from Germany, Italy and Japan were not ignored and the increase in spending on defence projects came to fruition and the RAE benefitted greatly. New developments meant more staff was needed and as unemployment had increased after the first war, recruitment in all aspects of defence and other jobs was vital as well as most welcome.

The war years – a genius at work!

Beatrice joined the **Royal Aircraft Establishment** (RAE) at Farnborough in April 1936 as a technical author in the Technical Publications Department. Here she revised or wrote instruction leaflets and maintenance manuals for aero-engines and aircraft. One of her publications was for the Bristol Pegasus II M3 engine.

She recollected an instruction about using dry ice – carbon dioxide - as a refrigerant to cool valve seats before inserting in a cylinder head, signifying that she added this instruction to one of her leaflets. It had been distributed without proof reading. Her suggestion was to hail an ice-cream van when needed! Once discovered, it did not go down well with senior staff, but did show her wicked sense of humour.

Beatrice's aim had been to investigate, research and develop aero-engines, but this was not to be at this stage in her life. Was it just a tiny step in that direction? *Perhaps.*

Paper and pen based tasks were a long way from the hands-on experience Beatrice had undertaken on carburettors etc. in Manchester. After all, she was a female and women were not very often employed in engineering because it was considered a job for men. *STEM-type employment and job satisfaction had to wait.*

Beatrice found herself working well away from the thrust of aerodynamics research; another disappointment for somebody of her calibre, ability and experience. The base for writers of engine and aircraft manuals was actually an old Post Office in the town where she was employed for approximately 6 months.

Boredom with her job was temporally lifted by a trip to Bristol to view a Pegasus engine being assembled and tested at full throttle. The engine was impressive and had a reputation for successfully powering the Royal Air Force's (RAFs) fastest twin-engined Boulton Paul Overstrand bomber as well as a bi-plane, the Vickers Vildebeest.

Sadly, she was prevented from meeting Roy Fedden, the Chief Engineer (and later knighted, Sir Roy) at the Bristol Aeroplane Company's engine department as he appeared to have an aversion to women anywhere in the factory. Beatrice recalled being removed from the premises if he was present and taken by car to another department building, the aircraft division, where females were employed. Here she could benefit from using the women's amenities and enjoy lunch with the girls, too.

Beatrice's persistence for employment in the research department at the factory site was finally granted in October that year. She was now able to work on aero-engines in the carburettor section, something she had experience with and an insatiable drive to explore and improve.

In 1937 the Nottingham Journal reported that Beatrice, along with another female, her friend Sheila, had been employed as *Air Ministry recruits'* to their staff.

Air Ministry Women

One of the most interesting new developments in women's engineering is the more general acceptance of women on the technical staff of the Air Ministry. Miss Hilda Lyon has been appointed scientific officer at Farnborough, and Miss Helen Grimshaw has also been given a post on the staff. Miss Beatrice Shilling and Miss S. E. McGuffie are also "Air Ministry recruits."

Nottingham Journal - Monday 01 November 1937, page 3

This was regarded as something quite unusual for a female, but what an achievement towards equality for women.

Beatrice's work included rectifying problems on a specially commissioned RAE carburettor for the Hercules aircraft engine including the automatic cut-off valve misbehaving and cutting out when it ought not to following a hard acceleration. This took until 1940 to solve, but once completed proved to be a reliable part when accelerated across the range, yet still required approval from the Ministry of Air Production prior to manufacture.

©Abebooks.co.uk

Dr Alan Arnold Griffith, an expert with a first class honours degree in mechanical engineering followed by a Masters and Doctorate from Liverpool University, originally joined RAE as a trainee in 1915. He went on to head the engine department in 1938.

As expected, Beatrice's day to day supervising boss was male. William Clothier, head of the carburettor division, worked well with her and they made an excellent team, both interested in work on developing injection carburettors, and in particular, finding a solution to eliminate icing in the throttle while flying at 20,000 feet (6.096 km).

Correspondence does not always receive the response you prefer

Beatrice continued to show just how talented she was by resolving further issues involving her ability in physics, maths – quantifying - and designing a mechanical solution. Her further STEM skills and knowledge ensured she could produce test situations, the results showing why the objects failed, if they did so. Beatrice's senior officers noticed, or at least those that mattered did.

Miss Shilling had applied for a more senior post earlier in the year; an upgrade from Assistant III to Assistant II. On August 5th 1937, the Chief Superintendent of RAE wrote to tell Beatrice of her success in obtaining this post, but in *'an acting capacity'* in the Engine Experimental Department. It stated her salary of £250 per annum and incremental date as April 20th and was signed on his behalf.

Immediately she saw the unfairness in the remuneration offer as it was lower than expected. Beatrice, of course, replied and pointed out the difference between what had been advertised and what was actually to be paid now. Clearly the pay offer was discriminatory.

"Sir, Vacancy 390/429A – Assistant Grade II August 1937

I beg to acknowledge with thanks your letter, referring to the above, dated 5th August informing me of my selection to fill one of the above posts.

The commencing salary of £250 per annum quoted in your letter disagrees with the advertised salary of £263-12-315.

May I be informed of the cause of this discrepancy.

Your obedient servant. B Shilling"

The initial letter informing her of her new position was signed *'p.p. Chief Superintendent, R.A.E.',* possibly by his secretary; 'p.p.' being an accepted shortened term for *per procurationem.* In business correspondence when signed by somebody other than the sender on his behalf, it means *'through the agency of ...'.*

Notably, the Superintendent, AH Hall, personally signed the reply, explaining himself by giving her an increase of £10 per year – *'an error',* but also pointing out regulations that may or may not be justified.

Beatrice did not argue the rights or wrongs of it at this juncture, but didn't forget or overlook it as in years to come would stand up for herself and what she believed to be fair.

At one stage, B was so disillusioned with working at RAE that, George and she decided to open their own business/workshops after the war, linked to bikes and cars but it never happened.

By November 1939, she had been promoted twice: once to Assistant Grade I in June 1938 followed by that of Technical Officer, which permitted her to run the team researching and developing carburettors.

Very quickly Beatrice became the leading specialist in aircraft carburettors. Edward Cameron, in The New York Times *(1910),* described the carb as *'the heart of an engine'* and went on to say if it wasn't functioning correctly then the car would not work effectively. It was imperative to get it working properly and this was something Beatrice excelled at, even though it was taking time and patience to research, problem solve and aim for a successful result.

School children, in design technology (DT) lessons, are encouraged to explore *'trial and error'* to problem solve when making artefacts; also in maths to problem solve. *All early STEM skills.*

It is characterised by repeated, varied attempts, both practically and through design in DT, which continue until successful or give up to seek support, occasionally through lack of time in the school day. *STEM is essential in today's schools as it provides great preparation for the future.*

Beatrice must have undertaken lots of trials and errors to improve the performance of her bikes and in her research projects, at university and work. She was meticulous and thorough in everything she did.

Beatrice fine tuning her bike
© Dennis Lock

Negative 'G' Simplified

During the Second World War, Beatrice worked on a serious problem affecting the Rolls Royce Merlin engines which were fitted to the allied Hurricanes and Spitfires during the **Battle of Britain in 1940**. The British engines, unlike those of the German planes, which benefitted from a type of fuel injection, would misfire or cut out altogether when a pilot was diving steeply, often causing deaths. This force was known as **negative gravity or 'g'**.

As an **aeronautical engineer**, Beatrice understood that there was a fuel surge – too much entering the carburettor and flooding it - which caused severe problems and needed an urgent fix – the negative 'g' issue. The balance had to be perfected – enough to power the engine, but not too much to flood it. Float type carburettors relied on gravity to work effectively.

Beatrice, later nicknamed Tilly by fellow colleagues, but not to her face, and her team worked tirelessly to resolve the negative 'g' problem. She never gave up. It was a year in the making though not a final solution at that stage by any means.

Initially she created a cone shaped device, but later, after thorough testing and still finding a few errors, it was redesigned. Eventually she came up with the design for a simple but resourceful device; a small brass disc with a central hole or cavity, which when fixed into the engine's carburettor was able to

© *Gordanohomefront*

induce fuel efficiency to the engine at the critical moment needed – the RAE restrictor.

Too much fuel would flood the float chamber, but not enough restricted engine power and a safe flight. The correct balance was crucial. Fitting it herself at times, Beatrice travelled from airfield to airfield across the country along with other females to ensure it was correctly installed. Again her self-discipline, painstaking and meticulous approach to her work was crucial in ensuring only the best would do. Men's lives depended on it.

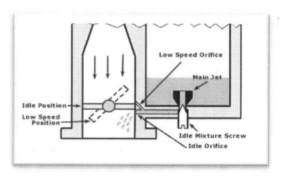

A very simple diagram of the orifice in different positions

A great advantage was not having to remove the engine to do so.

It has been likened to a washer or a pre-decimal 3d 'bit' coin with a hole drilled in the middle. It became known as Miss Shilling's or Tilly's orifice and after repeated testing – *trial and error* – demonstrated its effectiveness; an improved version was used on all allied aircraft with Rolls Royce Merlin engines.

Merlin engine © Peter Reese

Persistence towards perfection

Over time and further trials, it drastically reduced engine cut out and saved lives. It also meant that the British Spitfires and Hurricanes could dive and duck to avoid the German Messerschmitt 109s catching them in combat and therefore allowing the British to beat the powerful Luftwaffe.

© DERA Farnborough in Freudenberg 2003

The RAE carburettor which compensated for air temperature and pressure changes.

Beatrice didn't stop there, but continued to improve and develop the design in order to eliminate it entirely. Tilly, as she was nicknamed, was a fierce competitor, not only on the racetrack but also in the laboratory and no man stood in her way!

There are still about 50 WWII planes flying today in the UK for special events as well as those in military museums such as the Spitfire and Hurricane Memorial Museum in Ramsgate, Kent. The Hurricane fighter, first flown at Brooklands in 1935, is estimated to have been responsible for 80% of the enemy aircraft shot down in the Battle of Britain. One can be viewed in the Flight Shed at Brooklands. Amazingly, 20,334 Spitfires were built between 1936 and 1948, mostly to support the war effort.

Beatrice and her team must have been extremely busy sorting out their negative gravity problems in numerous Merlin engines.

Working on a Merlin engine

By 1942 the approved adaptations with the RAE restrictor along with essential advice was saving lives and helping Britain outdo the German bombers. Beatrice spent many a train journey as far as Scotland, fitting and supplying advice on engine carburettors and new developments. At last she was recognised for her contributions to the war effort, but only in a minor way.

In addition, planes were adapted for naval use on aircraft carriers. Initially, there had been problems with the Seafires missing the deck and going overboard or hanging by the catch wire when the hook hadn't engaged properly to stop the plane.

Later, Seafires *(named so from 'sea' and 'spitfire')* had folded wings and other adaptations to ensure the planes fitted their role at sea more precisely; they could be stored under the deck and play their part in saving lives. A number were Australia based where they undertook dog-fights with the Japanese *kamikaze pilots in the Pacific.

By 1945 Spitfires were engaged in several battles with the Japanese and succeeded in keeping them from invading India and Burma. They were used to drop 500 pound bombs at Sittang Bend in Burma resulting in 7,000 plus Japanese deaths compared to 95 British. Deaths were unfortunate, but it appeared a necessary task to ensure our freedom from tyrannical extremists who would not talk peace.

Dilemmas galore: choices to make, but it resulted in freedom for Britain and other countries in the world.

A Supermarine Spitfire © wikiwand.com

---

* Kamikaze pilots made deliberate suicidal crashes into ships or other enemy targets.

Did George challenge Beatrice to fly?

The **Tech-Flight scheme** at the RAE provided an opportunity for Beatrice to take up flying, logging some 200 hours but she never considered herself a worthy pilot. Being short at under five foot two, she had to build up the control pedals in order to reach them and this may have reduced her confidence slightly, although with racing that did not appear to be a problem; the exception being some bikes which she transformed. George, her husband, soared above her at over six foot.

A Yorkshire man by birth, he was a pilot in bomber command and flew for many extra hours during WWII, suffering from tinnitus – a hearing problem- and other medical issues in later life due to his flying. He was awarded and received the Distinguished Flying Cross for his

acts of courage and bravery.

Three out of every 100 night flights sent out on a raid did not return, often due to poor visibility and engine failure, so it was crucial that Beatrice and staff at RAE found solutions to negative 'g' and 'icing up' urgently.

Her team was working on another possible solution to 'icing up', something which became known as 'Tilly's Pepper Pot' to ensure the extremely low temperatures did not interfere with the pressure to the automatic mixture control. George's life and that of others mattered.

https://en.wikipedia.org/wiki/Distinguished_Flying_Cross_(UK)

Gallant pilots like George, ensured minimal damage was done to imperative sites such as London, Portland and Southampton as up to seventeen squadrons were deployed to demolish the Luftwaffe bomber formations hitting Britain.

Brave men indeed, while Beatrice and others worried about those urgent solutions needed to keep them safe.

Was learning to fly a challenge George set Beatrice in the same way she insisted he earned the coveted Gold Star medal for travelling at speed during racing at Brooklands?

If George's report on his elementary flying training at Wolverhampton Municipal Airport on September 29th 1943 is anything to go by, Beatrice may well have passed with considerable success.

FORCED LANDINGS:	Very poor
SIDESLIPPING:	Little idea
POWER APPROACH:	Judgement poor
LANDING:	OK but rather rough
INSTRUMENT FLYING:	Fair
GENERAL FLYING:	Rather Over confident
STYLE:	Poor
AIRMANSHIP:	Satisfactory
LOOK OUT:	Good
ASSESSMENT:	Just Average

A keen pupil who is handicapped by a lack of natural aptitude. He is inclined to get nervous on test and at present his flying fails to inspire confidence. He always has an excuse ready.

George was too old for Fighter Command, but did fly with the Bomber Command lads after further training on Airspeed Oxfords.

(in Freudenberg 2003)

Beatrice & George – Gold Stars abound

It is rumoured that Beatrice would not agree to marry her future husband, George Naylor, a mathematician she'd met at the **Royal Aircraft Establishment (**RAE) in Farnborough and on the race track, until he had attained the same Gold Star for equalling her speeds on the Brooklands track.

RAE badge for science knowledge & assistance © simanaitissays.com/

He was three years and eight months younger than B, having been born on November 8th 1912 in Normanton, a Yorkshire mining village.

George was a clever lad; excelled academically, particularly in maths and physics to win school prizes. The sports field was another area of success where he surpassed others and demonstrated his skills. Swimming was the same. Not only was he the school swimming champion but also became Head Boy in 1930, his final school year.

A fully funded scholarship to London University was the result of an exceptional Higher School Certificate in Yorkshire. George left University with an honours degree followed by attaining the status of Chartered Engineer before joining RAE as a Junior Scientific Officer in the Mechanical Test Department

It was here he met Beatrice and romance blossomed on the race track, too.

A work colleague, Brenda Rimmer, recalls how the three of them attended Farnborough Tech's evening class on aerodynamics.

On one occasion, George gave Brenda a pillion ride to the class, but she had to get the bus home because Beatrice and her new beau didn't return to class after a smoke break.

Brenda remarked that,

"I always thought it was a set up that evening."

This was early in 1936, but Beatrice did marry him two years later in 1938 at Aldershot Registry office on July 21st with minimal fuss and guests. According to David, her nephew, she had to seek permission from the RAE to marry George, but was permitted to do so and keep her job. Unusual at that time as many women had to resign once married, but war was fast approaching and Beatrice's skills were vital.

This ultimatum suggested that Beatrice may have had a dry sense of humour which could be witty and perhaps quite sarcastic, too. Her

nephew, David, reinforced this belief by recalling a detail about a Farnborough home.

"Early this morning I remembered Carfield was the name of Uncle George and Aunt B's house. Because it always had an old classic car in the run-in – a Lagonda and Fraser-Nash types."

© *Dennis Lock*

George, during training in 1943. He was trying out a

De Havilland Tiger Moth for size. He later flew with Bomber Command carrying out numerous raids against the Luftwaffe.

The Lagonda, pictured below, was modified and used on the racetrack. How amusing to think that they thought of their driveway as a *'car field'* for storing old classic cars! Humorous and ironic indeed. *Just like Beatrice to be sarcastic and witty for fun.*

© *LAT Photographic Archive in Negative Gravity (2003)*
Beatrice driving the winning Lagonda Rapier at speed during the five-lap Lagonda race at Silverstone in June 1957.

The interior of their home often housed engines and other car parts during modification and upgrading as was the case in Manchester when Beatrice shared a room with Muriel Shephard. While at University, they modified her bike in their shared room or at the Engineering Department's workshop.

Joan Foster, their neighbour, friend and racing fan recently confirmed this.

"Bee & George Naylor lived seven doors away from us in Ashley Road, Farnborough before they moved to Cove. My father also

worked at the RAE, in the radar department. My brother raced & we all went to meetings together. Their houses were always full of car bits & the dining room had a concrete floor to take the weight of their lathes!"

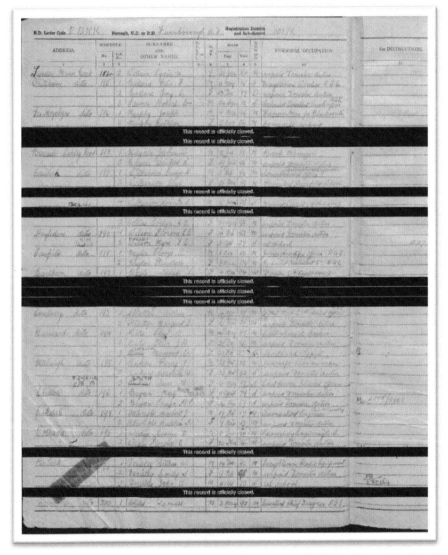

1939 Register showing Beatrice's & George's home at Carfield, also their racing friends the Derisely family at Purbeck. Officially closed records hide details of those still living.

David, B's nephew, recalls a large drill and other machine tools.

More recently their former home, Carfield, has been adorned with a Blue Plaque to mark B's achievements during WWII.

It was officially unveiled, followed by a buffet lunch celebration hosted by The Farnborough Society, on May 25th 2019.

In addition, a display of photographs and text recalled Beatrice's wonderful and life-saving accomplishments at RAE.

© *https://thefarnboroughsociety.org.uk/*

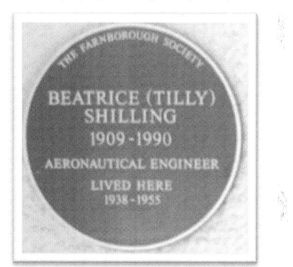

The Channel 4 programme *Inside the Spitfire Factory* told Tilly's tale and showed the Blue Plaque unveiling along with interviews.

Judith Derisely, her God-daughter recalled Aunty B with fondness.

"She wore thick corduroy trousers and a man's shirt with a cigarette hanging out of her mouth. Aunty B bought me presents such as chemistry sets and microscopes – children's ones – but also the only teddy I ever owned."(Inside the Spitfire Factory:5 28.10.20.Ch 4)

Love letters during the War

George did not enjoy his initial training or the living standards at his RAF base in Scarborough; a not so Grand Hotel by all accounts, although back in his native Yorkshire.

During WWII several RAF trainee cadets were based at the Grand. Anti-aircraft guns were mounted on the four turrets to defend the hotel and seafront. It had been damaged in WWI prior to Christmas 1914 when on December 16th approximately 30 artillery shells from German battle cruisers hit the hotel, completely destroying the restaurant.

Its relationship with the military continued in recent times when the SAS was based there following the siege of the Iranian Embassy in April/May 1980. The hotel was used to train SAS agents in covert exercises should there be any further terrorist attacks in the UK.

At the outset George regretted having joined up. Not only did he miss Beatrice, but expectations and conditions were not favourable even considering there was a war on.

A plaque pays tribute to the RAF Cadets

When writing to his wife he wondered,

"... why was I such a bloody fool as to join the RAF, but I won't say anything about that now. First, will you send my laundry immediately because I am running out of handkerchiefs."

Beatrice was expected to work full time and do his laundry as well! Devotion indeed, but it was expected in those days that women did all the household chores and in many cases still do today.

George found the conditions cramped and what appeared petty rules quite undesirable. Using the unlit back staircase was a pain as was sharing three toilets, often with no paper, between all stationed at that base. Sharing a wash hand basin between seven men, all of whom he disliked, believing them to be of low intelligence, peeved George, but that was not all. Rules about bed making and equipment storage irked George along with marching at 140 paces per minute. To crown it all, he was told Christmas leave was cancelled, but he did eventually manage to travel home and celebrate the festive season with Beatrice. Maybe George was very fussy or perhaps Beatrice and his mother beforehand spoiled him, although wartime conditions could be hard.

Beatrice, in her usual no-holds barred conversation with George told him to stay in the RAF in spite of his mental state and threats to get thrown out. Subsequently, his attitude towards his colleagues improved, especially after one made his bed up when they had not expected his return in time before lights-out to do so himself. They also allowed him first use of the washbasin each morning due to his slow approach in carrying out his ablutions. *They found him entertaining.*

Achieving full marks in his Morse Code test also gave George a boost, but he rarely wrote to Beatrice without a complaint or two as training was not completed until the following March. He fancied flying Spitfires and Typhoons, but did not fly until May 1943 and then it was learning in a Tiger Moth at No 10 Elementary Flying Training School at Fair Oaks airfield, Surrey.

© Dennis Lock

It has been speculated that Beatrice's marriage was not a strong one, but enforced separation for three years during the war helped stabilise it, along with regular correspondence between George and herself.

Her family would disagree; it was happy and fulfilling with much fun, risk taking and shared interests, both at work and play.

Their letters do declare love for each other and how being apart was difficult. Even when apart, they helped each other with work-related problems; George was not averse to advising Beatrice on how to try out solutions with the carburettor issues as well as their racing problems and resolutions; a great joint venture.

Both were extremely intelligent adults and there may well have been a competitive streak between them which could have caused a few problems, too, but 'darling' and 'sweetheart' were frequent endearments used regularly in their correspondence to each other. Matthew Freudenberg evidenced this in his book, Negative Gravity (2003)

Romance was certainly alive and kicking!

"Darling you know I love you very greatly, sufficient to encourage you in risking your neck in being a pilot or on a motorcycle more because I know you want to and will feel better if you are a pilot than because I want a pilot for a husband – you could become quite distinguished as a flutter-nark and stay a dart player for me.

All my love darling B"

Pressure of work at RAE, lack of sleep and George's training undoubtedly took their toll on both of them, never mind the dangers of war itself. B's unfortunate tone, too, could be mistaken in the short telephone conversations between them, but their correspondence throughout the war showed a deep affection and love for each other.

George's letter to B on Tuesday August 17th 1943 demonstrated his concern following their previous telephone call.

© Dennis Lock

"I am worried, what was the matter with you tonight? I know that if we had been lucky we should have been together tonight and I should not be sitting up in bed writing to you now, I should be in bed with you instead …

I love you more and more as time goes on and I miss you more and more as the days go by and I don't see you …

All my love, George"

In response Beatrice wrote,

"August 22, 1943

Carfield, Ashley Road, Farnborough

George dear,

If you write me letters like the one just before you phoned me twice last week, I shall start catching the train to Wolverhampton. Darling, it is a shocking business this being separated. I do hope to see you on Tuesday ...

I haven't seen you for 18 days, it is too long dear and between you and me I am going to make a job in Birmingham next week whether I see you or not this week ...

You know dear that I am too much in love with you to waste a 3 minute phone call being annoyed with you for going to a dance or something."

Being prepared to travel to Wolverhampton and Birmingham to be with George provides robust evidence of a strong relationship and love for each other even if a little turbulence caused unease at times.

There is no record of any children, and Beatrice was known not to be over fond of them, so both may have been more content in pursuing their personal interests in racing and working vocations or it just never happened. Children are expensive and time consuming, too.

George, in a letter to Beatrice, did suggest they would have to relinquish quite a lot to have children including Beatrice's career which she loved: their racing would be put on hold and they'd be broke for the next twenty years without her income never mind the expenses incurred in child rearing.

Beatrice, who had recently taken up flying appears to have made the decision for them.

Her body, her choice, her career at stake and again her sense of humour shows even if a bit more of a serious subject here. Writing to George she summed up her feelings aptly.

"I think all being well I'd rather have a Moth or a Magister (planes) than an infant. If I got a ground engineer's licence it shouldn't cost too much to run. Can I have one?"

Did she really have to seek George's permission or was she teasing him?

However, at one stage they did have a retriever puppy, Rita, a great comfort, and sometimes a welcome substitute to many childless couples. But her nieces and nephew, Nora's children, were always welcome and they were very fond of her; admiring her skills and her ability to turn her hands equally to many tasks.

In another letter to George, Beatrice explains that she had been out horse riding with Nora's children on Christmas Day. She fell, bumped her head and was perhaps a little light-headed afterwards, but the experience left her in little doubt that children were not for her. I suspect it was the bump on her head rather than the children!

"26.12.43

Dearest George,

...incidently, I am now finally and definitely decided that perpetuation of the race is a mistake."

Throughout the war Beatrice and her team continued with the demanding task of finding a solution to the negative 'g' problems along with the icing up of carburettors at high altitudes. This resulted in too high a number of planes and pilots not returning to base. Inclement weather caused poor visibility and crashes were inevitable.

Beatrice and a colleague, Bob Newton, flew in borrowed 1930s Fairey Battles and occasional Lancaster Bombers hunting down the cloud conditions where icing occurred, but were extremely limited due to other test departments or squadrons requiring the planes. She also regularly visited airfields to examine planes with carburettor issues.

George and Beatrice continued to correspond throughout the war, their mail sometimes being quite serious about work or other issues as well as being humorous, too, but their love was evident at all times.

Beatrice detested spiders, so much so that she chased them with a blowlamp ensuring they were cremated quickly.

"There are plenty of pockets of resistance in this house occupied by spiders so I decided a flame thrower was the only thing for under the sink." (In Freudenberg 2003)

Beatrice's sense of humour is again evident here, nevertheless the cruelty to our native eight-legged mini beasts is quite uncalled for.

Courteous speech was not something that came easily to Beatrice. She had little respect for unnecessary rules, regulations or primness which did not go down well with her employers or bosses. Beatrice could be quite offhand, had a brusque manner and was often impatient with those whose standards and efforts were less exacting than her own.

Although extremely clever and eventually reaching a senior position at the RAE, Beatrice did not go out of her way for advancement through being polite or thoughtful.

Had she sought promotion Beatrice could have enjoyed leading her teams with a bigger pay packet to cover her expensive racing habit costs, never mind cigarettes. She was a very heavy smoker. Many were at that time, being totally unaware of the impending health problems.

Critical of her superiors and being female did not predispose Beatrice to favourable positions of responsibility, but perhaps at times she preferred to be undertaking practical work and research rather than over-seeing those under her from an office environment.

Beatrice told George,

"I tend to be too rude to my superiors or ineffective. I doubt if I'll ever get to the standard of some old hands ..."

However, as mentioned earlier, she was promoted several times, particularly after her successes with carburettors and certainly deserved the recognition and additional pay, though received less than that paid to a male undertaking an equivalent job. *An extremely sore point!*

Beatrice was very much a *'doer'* and thought nothing of working late into the night – up to 19 hour shifts - far exceeding her normal hours to aim for a solution, but she also expected her team to do the same and was far from tolerant from those that abstained.

Fish and chips rewarded those that did the additional nocturnal shift, also trips to the pub for a pint!

Judy, her God-daughter, also recollected that B,

"Didn't suffer fools gladly and there were too many fools around. B kept solutions simple while others made them complex."

Beatrice adjusting her bike with George looking on.
© Dennis Lock

The couple's deep understanding of maths and physics often supported discussions and subsequent adjustments to their bikes and cars, preparing them for races. Mutual respect and a firm understanding at all times was paramount in work and play.

They were a highly successful and extremely well-co-ordinated crew of two!

Help on the Home Front

Following Beatrice's fall from a horse on Christmas Day 1943, she was beset with other problems, both medical and work-related. She was not used to being ill, so found it tough going. Not only was she dealing with George's complaints in the RAF and urgent problems at RAE, her own medical issues took their toll, so much so that she actually took a few days sick leave to help recover. However, she only gave in after feeling completely whacked following the repair to an external drain including mixing and laying concrete. This was on top of the assault her body had already taken from the horse fall.

Meanwhile, her friend Muriel Breed's husband, Desmond, a navigator, had been shot down over Holland in his Stirling on July 28th 1942. It was his first bombing mission and no trace of Desmond had been found. Muriel was devastated and firmly believed her premonition that he would not outlive the war, even though he was ten years younger than his wife. Sadly he had not met his two month old daughter, Elizabeth, before going down. She was destined to grow up fatherless. Life was so unfair, but more was to come.

Muriel and Elizabeth, now approaching a year old and known as Biddy, had been living in Eastbourne, a coastal town in the south of England and therefore a target for German bombers either directly or for off-loading their unspent cargo on returning to Germany. Their home had been totally destroyed. Muriel was desperate and contacted Beatrice for help, who readily agreed to her friend's proposition.

Both Biddy and Muriel moved into Carfield and life changed.

Beatrice must have relished the idea of having Muriel do the housework and return to a home-cooked meal in the evening. *Perhaps she helped with George's laundry, turning round his hankies quickly!*

Although Beatrice wasn't over fond of children and had decided

Muriel Breed née Shepard

not to produce any of her own, she welcomed both Muriel and Biddy to Farnborough, enjoying the female company, simple conversations and the more detailed discussions they had. They both enjoyed reading, too, so shared their favourite thrillers alongside some alcoholic drinks.

It was probably a great comfort to Muriel to be able to rely on Beatrice's support when it came to worrying about Desmond and his current unknown situation.

Biddy was the usual chatty toddler. Muriel possibly wasn't aware of her sounds or crying at times as she had suffered from a hearing loss due to the bomb blast in Eastbourne when her home was decimated. Biddy, however, told Matthew Freudenberg, that she recalls Beatrice taking her into bed and comforting her at night when Muriel did not hear her screaming. B obviously had a soft spot for children after all, especially when her sleep was disturbed.

Although good friends, they had different approaches to housework and argued over it, but B had it her way; after all it was her home and she could be quite obstinate to the point of being rude over anything she felt strongly about. Beatrice benefitted by having an adult around while George was away. Muriel was a shoulder to cry on over work issues and her husband's complaints, while B did the same for Muriel's worries over Desmond. Meanwhile Biddy played with Rita, the puppy. They shared each other's food when the adults were oblivious to the pair's developing friendship and activities.

However, by the end of the year there was good news. Desmond had survived the plane crash, but was in a prisoner of war (POW) camp in Stalag Luft III at Sagan, but at least he was alive and there was always hope that he would be returned to England after the war.

Muriel's niece, Rena Brewin, recalls,

"During his incarceration I understand that he was involved in the preparation of various escapes, including the famous great escape were over fifty POWs escaped through a series of tunnels. Fortunately for him, he was not one of those chosen to take part in the escape because nearly all of those recaptured were executed by the Gestapo."

Throughout the war years, George and Beatrice continued their discussions about the RAF flight problems he encountered and possible solutions in addition to those taxing B and her team at RAE. George was never really satisfied with his role, status or remuneration in the RAF and argued his case many times. He witnessed younger men with less qualifications than himself promoted to more prestigious positions, pay and pensions.

Bomber Command was his destination and no amount of arguments or letters changed that. Once he was stationed at Cranwell he gained his RAF Wings and automatically became a sergeant.

Beatrice felt it was *'a sad thing but I can't call my house my own'* as another friend, Bunty, moved in and took up with a man from RAE although she was married. Tasks were distributed and life carried on.

War – What is it good for?

Increasingly, Beatrice worked longer hours and returned home with research work to calculate and analyse. She wasn't remunerated in any way for her extra hours, so was absolutely fuming when her pay was docked for the two days sick leave she had taken the previous year. The Deputy Director of Research Engineering felt the brunt of her wrath.

"I have worked a greater number of hours than the number of hours in a full working week (no leave) with the present hours of attendance, and I believe that I am entitled to 36 days leave with pay."

Personnel did not relent. Nor did the department agree to reinstate her deducted payment or offer any extra for the additional hours worked. Beatrice was so cross that she decided to start up her own engineering company with George, once the war had ended. They both dreamed of building and racing bikes along with cars in the not too distant future. George, being unaware that their beloved Brooklands' track had been blown up to prevent the Luftwaffe using it as a strategic point in relation to London for bombing and also to extend the runway

for the Vickers' aircraft factory on site, carried on hoping for a quick end to his time in the RAF and the war.

Frank Borthwick-Norton and his wife Eva lived at Southwick Park, Southwick in Hampshire. It was their family home. *©https://historyarticles.com*

In the months leading up to D-Day it was decided to use the house as the main headquarters for the allied commanders, including General Eisenhower, who was the Supreme Commander, Admiral Ramsey, the Naval Commander in Chief and British General Montgomery, Commander in Chief of the Army. Only a few miles away from where Beatrice was born and the naval city of Portsmouth, it was strategically placed to do so.

Locals, who had noticed that rail services had been reduced to allow movement of both British and American troops, were also banned from the beaches at Southsea and along the south coast. Something secret was planned. Something big was planned, and something took place on June 5th 1944, the night before the D-Day invasion commenced.

More than 1,000 planes from the British Bomber Command – George's future section – bombarded the Normandy coast along with 1.300 US bombers from the Eighth Army Air Force taking

Planning the invasion at Southwick House

over to continue next day, providing cover for the boats approaching France.

George's training continued learning to fly various aircraft such as the Wellington bomber and Lancaster. When formal training was accomplished, on September 13th 1944, George and his crew joined 625 Squadron I Group Bomber Command in Lincolnshire.

He continued learning on the job when flying missions to Germany and other occupied lands, occasionally being told in the early hours that he was due to fly with the 625s later that day. One such flight, a daylight raid, on October 3rd, joined up with other Lancasters and Mosquitos to bombard the sea defences at Antwerp. An accurate attack, he delayed to ensure the cameras had recorded their success, only to take flak from the German's anti-aircraft fire which slightly damaged a wing and propeller. He relayed the tale to Beatrice,

"I was tremendously elated, for now I feel I have done something to justify my mistakes. (in Freudenberg 2003)

Although by the end of October, George had flown a third of the operations required to complete a tour of duty – ten in total – he was still unhappy at times, especially when a proportion of the armoured plating was removed from his and other Lancasters. This was meant to protect the crew. In addition, the bomb weight had been increased, taking the overall weight 1600 pounds in excess of that stipulated in the pilot's manual.

George's lack of confidence was further exacerbated by the need for the bombers to arrive in sequence, piloting much slower than normal, to ensure he was positioned correctly for the bomb run attack. On occasions his navigator had misjudged his timings forcing George to reduce his speed to under 140 mph so they all arrived together. They did not wish to present the Germans with an early warning by a random bomber appearing ahead of time. Sequenced attack was essential.

Ear problems saw George visit the medical officer who suggested removing him from flying duties, something he did not wish to do. The forces had a number of acronyms including LMF – Lack of Moral Fibre and George had no intention of doing that to be stigmatised as not coping. Beatrice suggested he saw a specialist but to carry on flying.

"Darling, I think you are right, if you can stand it you should complete your tour unless the ear specialist turns you down flat."

No appointment was offered, so George carried on flying regardless of his ear problems and fears with actual flying. The sooner his tour ended the better for him, but that was not to be. The powers that be at Bomber Command increased the tour number to 36 flights, just a few days before he had completed the original 30 operations. Worse still was the raid on Dresden, which left huge numbers of civilian casualties following the fire storm caused by the bombing. Not only that, but he was extremely fortunate to return to Blighty at all as his navigator misled the return route and they headed over Nuremberg. They had to avoid the flak during seven minutes of hell, but did escape, though not without problems. George was,

" ... expecting every minute to be my last."

His crew wanted him to sign up for more tours, but George declined and Beatrice agreed, knowing his squad had already lost 18 planes during that first tour. That and George's health, never mind fear, was more than enough to contend with.

In the meantime, less pressure was put on Beatrice at RAE, so she planned what business ventures they could undertake together once she left and George was discharged from the RAF. It had to incorporate their love of bikes and cars, but nothing was firmly decided although

Beatrice did buy the Lagonda Rapier and had a few wild ideas about how she would transform it after the war.

Celebrations went into overdrive throughout Britain and the

liberated countries in Europe when Germany's surrender was given by General Alfred Jodl to Eisenhower on May 7th 1945.

Jodl was a German Generaloberst who served as the Chief of the Operations Staff of the Oberkommando der Wehrmacht, the German Armed Forces High Command under Hitler.

© Wikipedia Alfred Jodl

The war in Europe was over, but carried on in Japan until they surrendered on August 14th. Desmond Breed had been released and George would soon be back at Carfield with Beatrice.

Prisoners from the Great Escape at Stalag Luft, Sagan have been remembered by many nations following WW2.

©http://aircrewremembered.com/stalag-luft-sagan-and-belaria-the-fifty.html

Beatrice - racing was her life at speed!

Incidentally, following the **Motor Car Act of 1903**, Britain was forced to a maximum legal speed limit of 20 mph (32 km/h) on public roads, but Beatrice hit the speed on private land at Brooklands 5.3 times faster!

Later in life, she almost killed herself at one point racing cars but had a hunger for speed. This never diminished.

Getting back to speed limits, there was concern that Britain's newly formed motor industry would be held back by their lack of ability to carry out sustained high-speed trials. On reflection, it needed someone like Beatrice and her challenging need for speed to lead the way forward! However, this role was reserved for men at that time – women were not employed as test drivers.

Although the concrete surface at Brooklands, built 27 years beforehand and opened in 1907, had lost its sheen and smooth top, Beatrice brought her 490cc overhead camshaft Norton to race in June 1934. Brooklands was in home territory in Surrey. However, working in Manchester her journey from there to Weybridge was a lengthy train ride via the guard's van. In addition Beatrice had to push her Norton between stations. Determination and sheer mettle ensured she made it every time. The bike was stripped back to the basics for racing, so could not be used on a public road, hence this difficult jaunt to Brooklands.

Beatrice was a new recruit to the British Motor Cycle Racing Club and this was her first attempt in that category at Brooklands. She had adapted her bike to comply with their rules as noted by Motor Cycle Magazine's report following the races.

"The fair sex struck another blow for recognition when Miss B. Shilling, who had done only about three practice laps in her life, finished sixth in her very first race and third in her second, lapping at over 90mph on a Norton tuned by herself. An M.Sc. of Manchester University, she had even made the pattern for casting of the elaborate aluminium fishtail, then finished the casting to shape."

Beatrice didn't baulk at taking on the experienced riders after this and went on to win her events. Despite gender discrimination at that time, once on the track, females held many record breaking attempts in car races, Gwenda Stewart, being one, though less so on bikes due to fewer being raced by women. Fanny Blenkiron, in April 1934, held the record for the first female to attain the coveted Gold Star at Brooklands for racing at 100mph.

Beatrice was next, achieving her Gold Star for an outstanding performance, beating the other bikers by lapping the track at 106mph.

She had further plans to super charge her Norton, but that had to wait. Major modifications took research, time and money and Beatrice was still submitting job applications.

By 1935, Beatrice continued to race with growing confidence and expertise. Her tinkering skills and proficiency with carburettors ensured she beat even the most experienced professional riders. In fact, that year is deemed to be her most successful on a motorcycle. So much so that Norton Motors wrote to not only congratulate Beatrice, but also asking for a photograph of her posing on her Norton to grace their 1936 brochure. She had just won the Hutchinson 100 Day race.

"We regard this as a very remarkable performance and indicates your prowess in the handling of your NORTON machine."

Beatrice agreed and the photograph was used to support a

©*Dennis Lock*

section on international racing successes.

Fortunately she started work in April 1936 at RAE, local to her. Although she now earned a salary, work curtailed her time modifying the bike and spending time on the racetrack. *Romance blossomed soon afterwards when she met George Naylor at RAE.*

George was not only an extremely proficient mechanic, but he also raced bikes at Brooklands. A relationship brooked in Heaven.

Brooklands continued to be the favoured track of George and Beatrice, both performing extremely well at times. Anne (Gladys Nancie), her sister, would occasionally accompany them as would B's friend Muriel and her beau Desmond Breed. The latter being a tall, strong and well-built man who soon became an expert at giving the Norton a push-start at the beginning of races.

That task had originally belonged to George.

They enjoyed their race days with family and friends, celebrating their wins and commiserating over their losses. The post mortem was always a time to discuss strategies and what could be achieved to improve the bike or their tactics before the next race. In addition, talks about the RAF men who took a fancy to Anne, a professional ballerina, were also discussed, with Beatrice giving advice in her usual curt manner.

Beatrice continued to dispense advice and strategies to her husband; tinkered with her bike and took great care of all its components to enable George to win a short, three-lap race without a super charger in the rain. April 1st 1938 was yet another Naylor success! However, throughout the summer months George didn't even manage to get placed as the Norton, minus the charger, failed to perform as effectively as usual. Other manufacturers' bikes, with super chargers, achieved success where they didn't. Super chargers on single cylinder bikes often caused problems and George never achieved his dream of breaking the 500cc Outer Circuit Lap record at an expected speed of around 120mph.

Poor weather did not deter Beatrice or George from racing but that autumn and winter provided other opportunities; initially there was important time to consolidate their recent marriage in July that year, embarked on after George gained his Gold Star. Another important pursuit was to undertake major bike modifications.

Work began on stripping the Norton back to basics and to create an almost new vehicle – one that boasted a super charger, made in their workshop, aka the back room, and fitted above the engine sprocket. A chain from the crankshaft was used to drive it. Further modifications included converting the petrol tank into a compressed air chamber to maintain pressure between the carburettor and the super charger

Instead of retaining the saddle it had been replaced with a Beatrice designed and manufactured fuel tank. The saddle was then relocated to above the mudguard on the back wheel. Beatrice's experience working on carburettors with Dr Mucklow in Manchester provided the inspiration for this design. As the fuel nourished the cylinder head, which was joined to the carburettor, compressed air from the super charger forced the concoction into the engine. Although it worked well in principle during her research days at university, the Norton faced many problems, all of which they admitted. It was back to the drawing board and more modifications.

By 1939 both avid bikers were fortunate to spend more time on the race track at Brooklands than in previous years. George demonstrated his mettle on many occasions while Beatrice ensured he was entered for most races. Although both very courageous and going all out to win, they didn't shy from admitting that the Norton was a scary beast when their laps were around 100mph or more.

Beatrice raced her Norton Manx until 1939, transforming it over time to improve performance and beat the lads. When war was declared, racing ended at Brooklands and the Norton was returned to a road machine to become Beatrice's chief means of transport for the next fourteen years. Both Naylors were heavily involved in finding solutions to other problems at RAE, so biking went by the wayside.

What would Beatrice choose today – would it be a **Harley, BSA** *(new 2021)* or another **Norton**?

Founded in 1898 Nortons were manufactured in several places including India and more recently in Donnington, Derbyshire. However that collapsed and the most recent Norton CEO, Dr Robert Hentschel, has been in post since June 2021.

Having established the key problems with Norton, he has outlined aspiring plans for the future, including new designs in his recently built state-of-the-art factory in Solihull. It is due to be officially opened in September 2021. Hentschel aims to build 5000-8000 bikes a year once his visionary plans have been developed and approved. Speaking of the future for Nortons he has stated,

"It's important to see a bike on the horizon and recognise it as a Norton. But it also has to be a sustainable approach."

Hentschel, a keen biker who bought his own Norton Commando 961 back in 2016 after visiting Donnington Hall, also hopes to reveal plans for racing soon and wouldn't rule out a return to the TT in the near future.

"I think racing is important to keep brand value high. Norton seems to be an undestroyable brand, but at some point we have to contribute to keep it where it is or to take it higher.

We want Norton to be using state-of-the-art technology and racing is part of that; it makes a statement. But we are not yet ready to make a public statement on this. We need to have a competitive product because I would like to win!"

More recently, MotorSport Vision (MSV) has purchased the freehold of the Donington Hall estate next to the race circuit, Donington Park. The beautiful Grade II listed Hall is currently being established as a prestige luxury forty-bedroomed hotel, with plans to

Donington Hall © IV 2021

open it in 2023. Hastings House will become the Donington Hall Motorhouse, home to classic road and racing cars as well as bikes and supercars.

The Lansdowne workshop will be available for high-end motor engineering businesses to prepare and maintain the vehicles kept in the new motor house, formerly Hastings House.

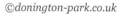

©donington-park.co.uk

Looking at the moves and plans, not only at Donington Hall, but also at Norton, it would appear that Beatrice's favourite bike, in some form or other, will take its place in history once again. Robert believes that his,

"over twenty-three years' experience in leading global automotive and motorcycle engineering organisations and now I am honoured to lead Norton Motorcycles as CEO at this exciting time of the company's rebirth. Norton has a remarkable history, and my role in this chapter is to help restore this iconic and much-loved marque to its rightful place on the global stage; it is a once-in-a-lifetime opportunity."

Read more at:

https://uk.linkedin.com/in/dr-robert-hentschel-1944aa44
https://www.motorcyclenews.com/news/norton-motorcycles-return/

However, will he have to compete with the new factory in Banbury building BSA motor bikes from 2021?

Locally in Waterlooville, where Beatrice was born, there is a Norton enthusiasts group where I have been fortunate to meet a couple of Norton Manx owners and bikes, including a 1947 bike at 73 years old!

John, the Secretary of a local Norton biking group arranged for a few of his friends to meet up. Geoff, who also worked at RAE, has a 1947 Manx and Roger a 1957 bike, but in great condition for their ages.

They very kindly trailered them to do a photo shoot and chat, but sadly it rained heavily, so we didn't get such good photos. However they loved showing off their incredible bikes and I had fun discovering more about both of them; working at RAE and racing.

Thanks, lads!

Both bikes – a 1947 and 1957 Norton Manx

Beatrice's final cycle- race was in 1951 aged 42. It was an off-road trial but not on her Norton. She had a modified Tandon with a two-stroke device engineered by Villiers and adapted by Beatrice herself. Sadly, she fell off the bike severely damaging her knee. The decision was made to end her motorcycling endeavours and adhere to car racing. From the mid-fifties both George and B raced a variety of cars with the British Automobile Racing Club (BARC), although retained a collection of bikes for their own personal use.

Brooklands - the history in a nutshell

Brooklands was briefly mentioned earlier as a favoured racing track of Beatrice and George. Today Brooklands is an aviation museum, housing examples of vintage cars, motorcycles and other forms of transport. Part of the former concrete track has been restored.

It originally opened in 1907 and held a 100 mile massed start cycle race. Road racing for cycles was not permitted on open roads at that time, so the Brooklands track was ideal: it was safe. The three and a quarter mile track surface was constructed of concrete with two straight runs, one slightly curved and joined by two semi-circular bends. To the spectators delight, high banking was visible from most areas on the track. It was considered safe at speeds of up to 120mph and rapidly became a very popular race course.

© Brooklands mass cycle ride

By the 1930s cycle races were common place there. A first for Brooklands was the trials to select competitors for the prestige World Cycle Championships to be held in Montlhéry in 1933.

1908 saw the start of motorcycle racing. Initially the numbers of spectators and participants were low, but over time this increased as did the speed of bikes and interest in racing. The track was built for speed; circuit experience was not a pre-requisite for using it. Sheer determination and pluck to *'have a go'* were more important, both of which Beatrice and George had by the tank full.

World War II that September put an end to racing at Brooklands and B's bike became her daily transport once refurbished to a legal road bike again.

Brooklands not only accommodated racing but also housed one of Britain's first airfields as it had been requisitioned by the War Office in 1914 for military use. By 1918, in addition to the racing track and aerodrome, it produced military aircraft such as the Wellington Bomber, but also the Viscount and VC 10, both commercial planes.

During WWI Brooklands was used to test bikes for use in the armed forces as well as holding race meetings for service men at that time. Sadly it was bombed by the Luftwaffe on September 4th 1940. It caused a substantial loss of life and untold injuries to many present on the site at that point.

© *Dennis Locke in James Holloway (2020)*

On re-opening following the end of the First World War, Brooklands was renowned for accommodating the fastest and best in motorcycle racing throughout the civilised world.

Races such as the Hutchinson 100 and Brooklands 500 miles races were very popular events and eventually led to women being included by 1928. *An opportunity Beatrice did not pass by when older.*

David, her nephew, explained the photograph of Beatrice on her Norton at Brooklands race track – three strong women.

"Beatrice on her Norton having a push-start at Brooklands from her friend Muriel Breed." *(née Shephard)*

Sadly, Muriel's spouse, Desmond, a great push-starter at races, was in the RAF and had been taken a POW in 1942.

© *Brooklands*

The last race at Brooklands was held by the Brooklands Automobile Racing Club on August 7th 1939. It was very well attended.

Refurbishing Brooklands – now STEM City

In 2015 Brooklands received a substantial grant from the Heritage Lottery Fund (HLF) of nearly £5 million to transform the listed Wellington Hanger into the Brooklands Aircraft Factory and restore part of the track to its former glory. It had been covered by an aircraft-hanger since 1940. This was removed, restored and re-sited. In addition, a plan to build a Flight Shed in which to store the museum's amazing artefacts of historic planes was enabled. Work has continued over recent years with private funding and a £1 million Government grant in addition to other donations.

©www.bbc.co.uk/news/uk-england-surrey

The Earl of March re-opened a refurbished Brooklands on June 17th 2017. To relive the first opening in 1907 a re-enactment of vintage cars drove around the track to emulate the original procession.

The aim of the project is to encourage and inspire generations of young people to take up STEM subjects as well as train volunteers to restore historic aircraft sympathetically and accurately to their former glory. *Adventurous plans for Brooklands and the race track!*

You may remember Beatrice's link with the Women's Engineering Society (WES) – Margaret Partridge gave her employment and encouraged her to undertake a university degree, a start to her STEM career, though not known by that term then. At the Brooklands' day you can meet, work with and be inspired by current female members of the WES. There are opportunities to tackle some STEM activities and win Brooklands' prizes, too. *Lunch is included as well.*

In addition, Brooklands runs a Saturday Science Club for any children 10-16 years of age who may be interested in STEM where they have the opportunity to build artefacts such as a Roving Robot over two weeks. The Brooklands' website advertised it as an opportunity to;

"Build an analogue robot that uses line-detecting technology to move swiftly along a marked path. On the way you will learn about electronics, motors and circuitry. You will get to use a soldering iron, wire up the robot and even get the chance to decorate your robot in your own style." ©*www.brooklandsmuseum.com/*

An update since lockdown from Brooklands:

"Saturday Science Club is currently being reviewed in line with government guidance and guidelines from the National Youth Agency. Updates will be posted to this website or our social media."

https://www.brooklandsmuseum.com/learning/teens/events-and-activites

Silverstone and Goodwood

Silverstone was the destination track chosen by B to race her modified Lagonda Rapier. Once again, speed was part and parcel of Beatrice's way of life and she raced around exceeding 100 mph.

By the time the Second World War broke out she had an exceptional reputation on the racing circuit, not only for motorbikes but also for racing cars such as her modified fixed head coupe.

©LAT Photographic Archive in Negative Gravity (2003)

The Naylors had been seeking a Lagonda since the war years but unfortunately didn't succeed in purchasing one until 1946. Initially, they agreed on a 1932 Alvis which George drove back and forth to his RAF base during the war until it became obsolete.

In fact two Rapiers were bought: one was basically an engine and chassis while the other was a fixed-head coupe. Beatrice explains their 4 years' of passion and dedication to their hobby.

"We stripped everything and rebuilt it to our limits. The body was scrapped, we built a 2/4 open aluminium body. Redesigned it and modified it slowly between races." (In Freudenberg 2003)

In fact, a substantial amount of work went into it, adhering to George's plan while Beatrice took care of the engine specifications.

Later, Goodwood at Chichester provided the main track for racing with some wins but mostly second and third places being the norm. Their purchase of a brand new Austin Healey Sprite in 1959, similar to the image below, was raced until 1962 with many modifications aimed at increasing its speed. It was tuned and raced by Beatrice and George. Mrs Naylor improved her speed and therefore time racing around the Goodwood track by 13.6 seconds, an impressive difference. Other than two practice laps on April 8th 1961, this proved to be her last race in the Sprite.

© www.sportscar2.com

Fortunately that was before the engine exploded and ended the car's life. George was driving. Even with his great skills as a mechanic he couldn't save the Sprite.

Sadly, Beatrice's car racing came to a hasty end following an extremely severe crash which seriously damaged her legs and restricted the blood flow in her circulatory system. She overturned the car at speed, fracturing bones in her shoulders and arms while crushing through her legs. Fortuitously they were not broken but seriously damaged. Had the car had a roll bar fitted, Beatrice may have come out less scathed that she did. George added that it was not her fault but that of a poor driver.

"Statements indicate that she was virtually pushed off course by a clot who could not drive and who was determined not to be beaten by a woman. End of her racing driving, or is it?"

Beatrice approached the Elva accident or *purposeful push* in a kinder manner.

"He was an ex-RAF pilot, so he was too busy checking the instruments to look where he was going."

Providentially he didn't do that when fighting the Luftwaffe or a Messerschmitt may have taken him out.

This was no hindrance to George who carried on racing regardless of potential dangers and blown up engines!

Here are just a few of the cars they had raced:

- Wolseley Hornet
- Morgan 4/4
- Alvis 12/60 saloon
- Lagonda Rapiers x 2
- Jaguar x 2, one of which George rolled, ending up hospitalised
- Mini – a Minor and a Cooper

There are many more and not all of them blew up either!

April 1966 was to witness George's final race. His Mini Cooper was propelled off the track during the race. Litigation was not permitted under BARC rules, so he did not get anywhere in arraigning the driver.

George was unable to work for a few months, but Beatrice continued transforming the Ginetta, possibly the G2 which was sold as a kit car to take Ford components and an aluminium body. No doubt Beatrice would have selected her own parts.

The latest Ginetta an AKULA – Russian for shark © Wikipedia 2021

Their second Jag, an e-type, was purchased by Beatrice in 1969. At that time, it was deemed the fastest race car in the UK. By the time the 1970s arrived, Beatrice was approaching her mid-sixties and George was only a few years behind her. Racing accidents had taken their toll on both bodies, although mentally alert and previously physically fit it was time to watch racing rather than personally partake.

Beatrice had experience of shooting and cleaning guns back in the days when her father was an expert shot at Bisley, so this became their main active pursuit. The Naylors had a number of rifles kept at home from during the war, although perhaps some had been handed in when the Government recalled them after it ended in 1945.

Small-bore target shooting took precedence, but they also *'knocked about'* in the local woods undertaking rough shooting with friends. True rough shooting was quite popular and most enjoyable for those who were keen on this type of sport, *though tough on the game.*

In a number of cases the grounds were mostly unkeepered and may have consisted of trees, scrub and bramble bushes, so a good gun dog was necessary to locate any game not visible to the naked eye. Game would be sparse, but the pleasure would come from not knowing what you might encounter; an odd woodcock, pheasant and other game birds may end up shot and ready for the cooking pot. Today there is less of this freely available for farmland and woods have been heavily cultivated; syndicate shoots are now arranged by landowners, never mind for health and safety reasons.

Recognition for Beatrice – at last!

Beatrice continued to work for the Royal Aircraft Establishment until her retirement in 1969 reaching a senior post and receiving a medal – the Order of the British Empire (OBE) in the News Year's Honours List 1948/9 for her efforts during the war.

In 1969 she was awarded an honorary doctorate from the University of Surrey: was a chartered engineer and a member of the Institution of Mechanical Engineers in addition to the Women's Engineering Society.

According to the Engineering Council, chartered engineers, *(Wikipedia 2018).*

Beatrice receiving her Honorary Doctorate from Professor Lighthill © surrey.ac.uk

"Are characterised by their ability to develop appropriate solutions to engineering problems, using new or existing technologies, through innovation, creativity and change. They might develop and apply new technologies, promote advanced designs and design methods, introduce new and more efficient production techniques, marketing and construction concepts, pioneer new engineering services and management methods."

There is no doubt that Beatrice Shilling achieved that and more. She certainly deserved her honorary doctorate in December 1969 awarded by Professor Lighthill from Surrey University.

.

Rockets and bobsleds

After the Second World War, Beatrice worked on a host of projects, including rocket fuel research, the ramjet engine, and the Blue Streak missile system. Its role changed to become the first stage of a satellite launcher, but was eventually removed from the space race due to costs. A few of the remaining rockets are held in museums, including the National Space Centre in Leicestershire.

1960s Woomera, Australia, Blue Streak rocket testing ©@1steviekilne

In their spare time both Beatrice and George continued to race cars and motorcycles until their health prevented it. At one point, she also lost a tooth or two following a racing accident.

Beatrice must have been in her element researching rocket fuel. It didn't stop there for Beatrice either. Another enterprising adventure was designing a bobsled for the RAF Winter Olympics.

The bobsled was designed and built outside normal working hours at Farnborough, but never made it, mainly due to under funding and the modifications needed to comply with regulations. Limited testing was undertaken in St Moritz, but it clashed with another major racing event. Although Beatrice continued to seek funding to modify and improve the design none was forthcoming, so her dream of a new racing adventure, as a spectator, never materialised. However, today, funding would have been available from sources to promote their businesses.

Retirement doesn't mean sit back and relax!

Beatrice had fun in her retirement in a variety of ways. You can guess some of them! During it Beatrice carried on providing expertise via consultancy work; was a keen and experienced pistol shot, perhaps originally linked to those younger days cleaning her father's rifles, but also carried on her love of bikes and cars.

She raced around Surrey in her classic Triumph Dolomite Sprint until no longer able to do so. Chronic pain made movement difficult in her later

©*inventricity*

years. It must have been so frustrating laced with sadness for somebody who had such an active brain and once an energetic and vigorous body that didn't know how to stop, but was forced to do so.

Beatrice also enjoyed reading and watching motor sport on television. Although she didn't compete in the 1967 Grand Prix herself, she had the opportunity to investigate the F1 driver Dan Gurney's engine which had serious mechanical issues. These prevented him from participating and achieving a successful win.

Occasionally she entertained family members and kept in touch with a few close friends, too. Dennis and Anne (Gladys), her sister, being regular visitors along with social calls from her nieces and nephew.

It was good to keep in touch, catch up with family events and discover what David, Janet, Marian and their families were doing.

© DERA Farnborough in Freudenberg: Negative Gravity (2003)

Beatrice looks closely at the Gurney Weslake engine. Mechanical troubles prevented Dan Gurney from finishing among the leaders of the 1967 Grand Prix World Championship. *DERA, Farnborough*

Wretchedly and probably quite painfully, Dr Beatrice Shilling died aged 81 on November 18, 1990 from cancer of the spine.

She smoked heavily, but no evidence suggested that cancer affected her lungs, although she had spent years fighting off hacking coughs to no avail.

According to Dennis, Beatrice's sister Nora had orthopaedic problems due to osteoporosis, a loss of bone density and strength, resulting in her body *'shrivelling pathetically'*, and sadly dying in pain, too. His first wife, Anne (Nancie), B's sister, lived until she was 103!

Longevity appears to be prevalent in their family, though sadly not for Beatrice.

This remarkable female engineer, who was born and raised in Waterlooville, Hampshire, until five years old, played an instrumental role in defeating the Nazis during the Second World War having invented her 'orifice', a safety device, for the carburettors of Hurricane and Spitfire Merlin engines. This RAE restrictor saved so many lives.

A few years ago, Beatrice was featured in Winchester's Heritage Open Days during September 2018, where she was celebrated as an *'Extraordinary Woman of Hampshire'.* Notable local women from both the past and present were recognised for their achievements.

©Brooklands – Beatrice's driving licence

Beatrice making history all over again!

Earlier I said Beatrice's birthday would go down in history. Today, International Women's Day (IWD) is celebrated on March 8th – Beatrice's birthday!

The campaign theme for 2021, was;

#Choose To Challenge

IWD believe,

A challenged world is an alert world.

And from challenge comes change.

So choose to challenge!

It is a day to celebrate female achievements across the world, especially, like Tilly, in what was considered a man's world. IWD aims to seek a more balanced world where both male and females are treated equally.

The idea to promote it as an international event came from Clara Zetkin in 1910. She proposed her notion to one hundred women from  seventeen different countries, all of whom, were attending an International Conference of Working Women in Copenhagen. They backed her unanimously and it became an annual event from 1911 in Austria, Denmark, Germany and Switzerland.

© www.bbc.co.uk/news/world

In addition the IWD's purpose is to achieve an increased awareness to avoid prejudice as well as improve working and living environments that are much better for all regardless of nationality, gender and birth. Although only one day a year is allocated to celebrating this, work carries on every day to raise consciousness and action. It is a global campaign with the same themes worldwide. The UK's Suffragette movement is also included but it began ahead of IWD.

Beatrice 'Tilly' Shilling would have supported IWD without a doubt. As an early pioneer for women's rights in the workplace, society and life in general, seeking a more balanced approach for women would have been at the forefront in her eyes. *Almost a century later women have still not achieved equality in many aspects of life.* During her lifetime, Beatrice proved she could excel at what men did and more; not only in the work place but in play, too. She believed everybody had a talent – both male and female - just waiting to be discovered and nurtured. For example, she aided her niece, Janet, to become a teacher by supporting and helping her during training. *Remember, Beatrice was a first class mathematician and her expertise would have been a tremendous help to Janet, along with her other skills.*

There are many women out there setting extremely high standards and showing the world what they can achieve. Equality should be a two-way objective for both males and females. Diversity needs celebrating and shouted loudly from the rooftops.

Beatrice - our local icon and star

Locally, Beatrice's name has been carved in stone to celebrate her achievements. Recently constructed, Beatrice is remembered as a residential development for the over sixties was completed in London Road Waterlooville, and aptly named Shilling Place in her memory.

Since writing began on this book, the local Library in Waterlooville has commemorated Beatrice with a plaque and ceremony to mark her brilliance and relationship to the town. Havant's Lord Mayor led the ceremony.

"Local inventor, engineer and racing driver, Beatrice Shilling OBE, will be commemorated with a plaque at Waterlooville Library. The Mayor of Havant will officiate."

(The News March 8th 2019)

Slightly further afield in Southampton, the 2Time Theatre group at the Nuffield Theatre produced *'Tilly and the Spitfires!'* A play about Beatrice and her accomplishments. *(2timetheatre.weebly.com/)*

Has Beatrice inspired you to become a STEM engineer?

Beatrice's name and achievements are slowly getting out there and it is about time, too. Beatrice was such an inspiration to all females, especially those who enjoy tinkering in engineering, STEM subjects and can perhaps build a career in that field.

Manchester University, where Beatrice originally undertook her degree, now offer a bursary of £1000 or £2000 in her name. It is payable in the first year of study from 2021. *(It was £6000 a few years ago but conditions have changed.)* The Beatrice Shilling Scholarship is open to United Kingdom (UK) fee paying female students that have applied to the School of Electrical and Electronic Engineering at The University of Manchester via the Universities and Colleges Admissions Service. (UCAS) *www.eee.manchester.ac.uk/study/undergraduate/fees-amd-funding*

Coventry University has also recognised the impact Beatrice made by naming their new engineering and computing building after her. The building will be used to highlight STEM subjects – Science, Technology, Engineering and Maths. It was recently constructed by Speller Metcalfe at a cost of £27 million. *https://spellermetcalfe.com/project/beatriceshillingbuilding/*

The Royal Holloway University of London (RHUL) has commemorated Beatrice in their STEM funded building aiming to achieve gender equality. It is estimated that it currently reaches out to 30% of their female students. A percentage well above the female average of uptake in electrical engineering.

Professor Hogg, from RHUL, has stated,

"It's a building you want to be in…it's a place where you feel stimulated to be creative."

https://stridetreglown.com/projects/the-beatrice-shilling-building-rhul/

The Beatrice Shilling Science Building, at their Egham campus was officially opened on 27 March 2019 by Professor Dame Ann Dowling, President of the Royal Academy of Engineering.

Incidentally, Beatrice's brother-in-law, Dennis attended the ceremony, too, along with his second wife.

"Jane (my wife now) and I had an interesting time as guests of Royal Holloway, Egham for the official opening of The Beatrice Shilling Building recently."

At the time of writing the UK is 20,000 short of engineering graduates with fewer women working in this area than anywhere else in Europe. *20,000 short – this is ludicrous.* The idea behind the new building is to provide first class education to students and minimise this shortfall while encouraging more women to become the next generation of electronic engineers and scientists. Innovation and expertise is crucial to train the world-class engineers for the future. In the UK we really do need to be able to compete in the international market.

www.royalholloway.ac.uk/about-us/news/royal-holloway-officially-opens-its-new-state-of-the-art-science-building-the-beatrice-shilling-building/

Have a drink at the Tilly Shilling

Not to be outdone with educational establishments, Wetherspoons, a chain of public houses, pubs to you and me, opened a new one in Farnborough during 2011. It was aptly named the Tilly Shilling to pay tribute to Beatrice with Spitfire controls for door handles and other artefacts from the 1930s including a Spitfire blue print, aircraft-style seats and a propeller on the wall. It was certainly worth a visit.

Apparently, the nickname 'Tilly' was a bit of an unkind gesture; the name never being used to her face as it was an unflattering reference to her dress sense – that of a rather plain dame.

A Tilly, from the word utility, was a vehicle produced cheaply based on existing car designs during WWII and used by the armed forces at that time.

In wartime, 'tillies' were a low-powered British-made pick-up truck used

© en.wikipedia.org/

by the military such as this Hillman based car for the Navy. Again, a bit of an insult to such an intelligent aeronautical engineer. No man would have been insulted in that manner, which again shows the rather urgent need for gender equality in all walks of life.

Beatrice's memorabilia

Brooklands was Beatrice's favourite track and the world's first purpose-built motor racing circuit so it seems fitting that the Gold Star will now feature in a display at Brooklands Museum, together with the other memorabilia. Andrew Lewis, Museum Curator commented,

"We are delighted to be able to display Beatrice Shilling's badges at the Museum. Her work on the Rolls-Royce Merlin engine which was fitted to many Brooklands built aircraft, combined with being the first of only three women to win a Gold Star makes her a particularly interesting character in Brooklands' history.

https://antique-collecting.co.uk/2015/08/06/beatrices-brooklands-badges-sold/

Beatrice Shilling Timeline

1909: Beatrice was born at 4 Sidney Villas, 236 London Road, Waterlooville, Hampshire to Annie (Nancy) and Henry Shilling on Monday March 8th 1909

1914: The Shilling family moved to Surrey when Beatrice was aged five.

1921: Beatrice and family lived at 65a South Street, Dorking, Surrey. She won the Meccano competition with her moving 'Spinning Wheel' entry in the section for competitors aged between 10 to 14 years of age.

1923: Beatrice bought her first motor cycle an Enfield 2-stroke.

1924: As a teenager Beatrice decided she wanted to be an engineer.

1926: On leaving school Beatrice took up an electrical engineering apprenticeship with Margaret Partridge.

1929: Beatrice borrowed £1000 for fees and enrolled on an Electrical Engineering degree in Manchester as one of only two women students. At some point during the next three years Beatrice rode a 1928 Matchless motorbike, racing it in the Peak District as well as a Tandon, a bike produced for the Indian market.

1931: Beatrice shared a room with Muriel Shephard, a biking friend at Victoria Road, Whalley Range, South Manchester.

1932: She finished her degree (2nd Class) in Electrical Engineering then followed it by undertaking an MSc in Mechanical Engineering.

1933: Beatrice completed her MSc in Mechanical Engineering at Manchester. She began investigating the behaviour of super-charged cylinder engines with Professor Graham Mucklow in Birmingham.

1934: Beatrice started racing at the Brooklands track with a Norton M30 500cc motorcycle, adding a supercharger and lapping the Brooklands track at 106mph. She was awarded the prestigious Brooklands Gold Star for outstanding performances in track and road racing.

1936: The Royal Aircraft Establishment (RAE) in Farnborough employed Beatrice on April 25th as a Technical Author, where she later became a leading specialist in aircraft carburettors.

1938: George and Beatrice wed in Aldershot during September of that year then went to live at Carfield 10 Ashley Road Farnborough.

1940: Beatrice researched and invented the RAE restrictor – Tilly's orifice - to improve fuel problems in Spitfire and Hurricane engines during the Battle of Britain. Although her design reduced the engine stoppages – negative gravity - it did not stop them completely.

1942: She continued, with her team, to improve the design and Rolls-Royce incorporated their final design: the RAE anti-G carburettor, in 1942.

1947: Awarded the OBE for her work during World War II.

1951: An accident, damaging her knee, forced her to give up bike racing.

1955: Beatrice and George moved to Ravenswood Prospect Road Farnborough – it has since been demolished.

1956: Beatrice joined the Institute of Mechanical Engineers as an Associate Member which gave her the qualification of Chartered

Engineer following her promotion at RAE to Senior Principal Scientific Officer (Special Merit) in the Mechanical Engineering Department. *(Part of her application below © Institute of Mechanical Engineers)*

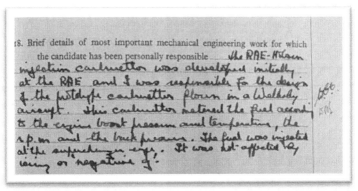

1962: A serious accident, while motor racing at Goodwood and resulting in the breaking of many bones which also prevented normal circulation, led Beatrice to finish motor racing.

1965: She wrote a summary of her car racing career for the newly formed British Women's Racing Driver's Club. The last entry read:

"23rd June 1962. Members BARC race, Goodwood. Elva Mk VI Sports Racing Car. 1m 48secs in practice. Standing lap in 1m 50 CRASHED. Car written off, driver nearly."

(www.bwrdc.co.uk)   *Car parts of the Elva and others at Carfield ©Roger Dunbar*

1969: Beatrice retired from full time employment at the RAE but still continued with consultancy work there and elsewhere. She also received her Honorary Doctorate at Surrey University in December 1969.

1990: Beatrice died from spinal cancer but was survived by George who lived for a further six years.

Aeronautical engineer Beatrice 'Tilly' Shilling, at the Royal Aeronautical Establishment at Farnborough in The Petersfield Post (2018)

Beatrice Shilling (Naylor)

OBE PhD MSc CEng

1909 – 199 Aeronautical engineer Beatrice 'Tilly' Shilling, at the Royal Aeronautical Establishment 0

doing what she loved!

© Dennis Lock

A note from the author: What can you do?

Don't be modest, celebrate your achievements and go out for what you want in life. Beat or at least equalise in your ambitions with the males of this world! There is plenty of talk on the web about including women and minority groups in having equal opportunities, but it is not happening fast enough. The IWD website states,

"Gender parity will not be attained for almost a century. There's urgent work to do – and we can all play a part." (2020)

The technology industry is amongst the poorest for diversity and equal opportunities when it comes to selecting women in senior posts never mind on their boards of directors. Sadly, gender issues reign.

"I raise my voice, not so I can shout, but so that those without a voice can be heard. We cannot succeed, when half of us are held back." Malala Yousafzia *(2016)*

We need to change that; whether you are male or female, like Beatrice, influence the powers that control our workplaces and schools. *STEM for all! Equality for all!*

* Show them your skills

* Celebrate diversity

* Be proud of yourself!

* YOU CAN DO IT!

It may only be a tiny objective, but it could mean the world to you or your children. Try it!

Glossary: including those terms known by their abbreviated form

*Ada Lovelace - the daughter of Lord Bryon, a famous poet, was a talented mathematician and is said to have written instructions – algorithms - for Charles Babbage's Different and Analytical Engines: early calculators and computers in the 1800s.

*Ambidextrous – means being able to use both hands equally well to write, draw and manipulate objects, usually with skill.

*Aeronautical engineer(s) – would undertake work on the different components that make up aircraft and their systems e.g. fuel or propulsion etc. Environmental issues are of grave concern and increasingly requires expertise is reducing the impact of flight pollution. More recently the term used would be an aerospace engineer, working on planes or space craft.

*Babbage Charles – was born in 1791 and was fascinated by maths from an early age. He taught himself algebra and used his skills to explore technology and his *'computer systems'* of that time; the most famous being his Difference Engine to calculate tables followed by the Analytical Engine, a fore runner of computers. Due to lack of funding it was never completed.

*Battle of Britain in 1940 – Hitler wanted to invade Britain hoping Churchill would agree a peace arrangement, but that did not happen. The battle was mainly airborne across the south coast of England during the summer and autumn of 1940.

The RAF ensured the Germans did not gain control of our air space. Although it did not finish the war it helped considerably in preparing for Operation Overlord, the 1944 battle in Normandy to overcome the Germans occupation in Western Europe and end the war.

*BSA (Birmingham Small Arms Company Limited) - was a group of British industrialists who manufactured a whole range of products including firearms for both leisure and the military. In addition they created bicycles, motorcycles, cars, buses and tools of many descriptions. Indian billionaire Anand Mahindra has a 60% stake in BSA and hopes to start building bikes in the UK by mid-2021.

Computing at School - Computing is our future, so every child needs the best teaching and first-hand experience it can receive to ensure they are ready for today and what is to come. CAS is an organisation incorporating teachers, university staff, IT experts and developers as well as other professionals and parents to support and equip schools to promote and make certain their passion for first class computer education happens. They hold local meetings in schools and universities where members share their expertise, often by practical means and first-hand experience. This can then be cascaded to schools.

Daisy the Dinosaur – an internet based simple coding game for young children to make her jump, spin and grow etc.

*Driver and Vehicle Licensing Agency (DVLA) - is based in Swansea, Wales. It holds over 48 million drivers' records and 40 million records of vehicles, including motorbikes, lorries and cars etc. on its database. In addition it collects the road tax due on vehicles. Specialist number plates, such as those with unusual registrations can be purchased here.

People who have not paid the due tax are followed up and can be fined if caught. In addition it deals with medical issues for drivers to ensure they are safe to drive. The staff also record and mark up licenses with penalty points etc. should a driver have committed an offence such as speeding. Another duty is to assist the police in any crime related issues involving drivers or vehicles such as accidents or thefts.

*Grace Hopper – was a USA computer scientist who worked on the Harvard Mark 1 computer. She was a Rear Admiral in the Navy and helped decode enemy messages. In addition she was a maths professor and wrote some of the first code for computers leading to COBOL; standing for COmmon Business Oriented Language.

*LegoWeDo2 – creates opportunities to combine science, technology and computing skills in an enjoyable way to make working Lego models. Using code on a tablet or similar device and following web-based instructions to create a moving, script-controlled model, children can explore trial and error; check out solutions and explore scientific options which develop their problem solving expertise in a fun way. It provides hands-on experience, as well as aiding computational thinking skills through asking scientific and computer based questions linked to their enjoyable experimentation. https://education.lego.com/en-gb/ & *https://education.lego.com/en-gb/homeschool*

*Meccano - Frank Hornby, manufacturer of the famous trains invented Meccano around 1898. It was a construction kit of metal strips, nuts, bolts, plates, wheels, axles, angled girders and gears to build working models. It is still much sought after today but it is now mainly manufactured from plastic rather than tin plate.

*MOT - The Ministry of Transport (as it was) test checks that your vehicle meets road safety and environmental standards. It is essential once a car is three years old and must be tested and pass every year before legally being allowed on the road.

*Motor Car Act of 1903 – was introduced by Parliament to increase speed limits from 14 to 20mph as well as vehicle registration which required each vehicle to show number plates. Drivers paid five shillings to obtain a licence, although no test was required. Any reckless driving resulted in a court appearances and a fine.

*Negative g - Gravity is a force of attraction that exists between any two masses anywhere in the universe. The bigger the object, the greater the gravity – so the Earth's is greater than the moon's. We say that the Earth's standard form of gravity is 1G, equivalent to travelling at 9.8 meters per second. **G-force** is a force created by something travelling at a speed of more than 9.8 meters per second and can act against gravity. An example would be travelling on a rollercoaster.

Negative G-force is when something accelerates downwards with the pull of gravity. In early Spitfires, fighting manoeuvres caused a rapid change from positive to negative G forces which stopped the carburettor functioning properly. There was either too much or too little fuel, so sometimes the planes crashed. Positive G-force is when something accelerates upwards against the pull of gravity.

*Norton Commando – a British built motorbike that is attractive and holds the road well. Although very expensive compared to Japanese bikes, it does not have unnecessary devices and additions.

*Norton Manx 500 - is a British racing motorbike built between 1947 and 1962. There has been a Norton in every Isle of Man TT race since it started in 1907 through to the 1970s. You can still purchase a Manx as it is sought after worldwide. Nortons have an enormous fan base. *Have another look at the images of the 1957 Manx and also the older model from 1947 – one of the first ever made! (Page 98)*

*Podcast – an audio/sound file that can be downloaded or uploaded to the internet.

*Professor Mucklow – was appointed assistant lecturer in engineering at Manchester University in 1922, and in 1926 later became a lecturer. By 1940 he was selected as Chance Professor of Mechanical Engineering at Birmingham University, one of his interests being the carburettor. *Beatrice worked with him.* Currently, Birmingham University offer a prize in his name for the best submitted project in the final year of the Bachelor of Engineering programme.

*Royal Aircraft Establishment (RAE) - was a British research centre based in Farnborough, Hampshire specialising in aircraft. Much scientific and mechanical work on all sorts of aircraft and components etc. has been carried out here, especially during WWII. Experts are also set the task of establishing why aircraft failed or sustained accidents. At one point the Ministry of Defence (MOD) was responsible for it. However in more recent times it is was known as the Royal Aerospace Establishment and now forms part of the Defence Research Agency.

*Royal Enfield – Based in Redditch, Worcestershire. The Enfield Cycle Company made motor cycles, bicycles, lawnmowers and engines. Originally they made weapons as their logo shows a cannon with the moto *"Made like a gun"*. Their brand name Royal Enfield was licensed

by the Crown in 1890. Currently the bikes are made in Chennai, India.
www.royalenfield-uk.co.uk/history

*Sir Lancelot du Lac – was it a fairy tale, Celtic legend or really true? It was said that Lancelot was the son of King Ban of Benwick and Queen Elaine. He was also the first knight of King Arthur's Round Table and the greatest fighter of all the knights. Although it may well be a myth, throughout the centuries King Arthur, Guinevere and Lancelot have held our interest via movies and stories and will do so for many more years to come.

*Site of Special Scientific Interest – is an area of protected land or water as defined by the European Union's Habitats Directive because it contains unique species or habitats of high scientific value for conservation. Rules are in place to register and protect such land and species.

*STEM – Science, Technology, Engineering and Maths, subjects taught at school, clubs and further education colleges to encourage an early interest in developing the WOW factor of STEM.
The aim is to promote future careers enabling the UK to have a strong position in world markets through links with industry. The arts have been added in some cases, so now we have STEAM.

*Stemettes – is an organisation that engages first-hand to inspire young girls from 5 upwards with technology, maths, science and engineering (STEM). The purpose is to encourage them to change the world's attitude to become more gender neutral by increasing the number of females in these subjects. The girls hold events all over the country in schools, clubs and halls. Dr. Anne-Marie Imafidon's team's expertise taught some of my pupils how to legally *'hack'* websites such as the BBC by overlaying a *'false homepage'* through coding. It was fun!

*Universities and Colleges Admission Service (UCAS) – is used by students to apply for an undergraduate university place in the UK.

*V Tech-Flight scheme – A scheme set up at the Royal Aircraft Establishment to enable competent aircraft staff to learn how to fly aircraft.

*Women's Engineering Society – The organisation celebrated its centenary in June 2019. When established in 1919 it was intended to improve equality for women in engineering, especially during the war years. When men returned from war many women returned to the kitchen. The men re-established their roles in the work force. 100 years later only about 14.5% of the engineering work force are women.

As reported in June 2021 by Engineering UK:

- Women make up 14.5% of all engineers
- This represents a 25.7% increase in women in engineering occupations (compared to a 4.6% in the overall workforce) since 2016.
- The number of women working in engineering occupations has risen from 721,586 in Q2 of 2016 to 906,785 in Q3 of 2020.
- This is an increase of 185,199 women in engineering occupations between 2016 and Q3 2020.

The full report will be published in the autumn of 2021. WES

Bibliography:

Alan (2018) Alan's Meccano: *Image of old Meccano 1911-12* Available from: www.alansmeccano.org (*Accessed: March 2018 & January 2019*)

Austin Healey Sprite (2020) *Image of a similar car to Beatrice's* Available from: www.sportscar2.com (*Accessed: Sept 2020*)

BBC (2017) *Beatrice Shilling: Pioneering engineer's genius 'helped win World War Two'* Available from: www.bbc.co.uk/news/uk-england-manchester-40267364 (*Accessed: December 2018*)

BBC (2020) IWD 2020 −*History, strikes and celebrations: When did it all start?* Clara Zetkin Available from: www.bbc.co.uk/news/world (*Accessed: November 2020*)

BBC (2017) *Brooklands racetrack finishing straight re-opened* Available from: www.bbc.co.uk/news/uk-england-surrey-40314868 (*Accessed: Sept 2020*)

Bisley (2018) *Bisley Shooting Range* Available from: www.bisleyshooting.co.uk/ (*Accessed: 2018*)

Blake-Coleman Barrie (2016) *The Fabulous Tilly Shilling* Available from: www.inventricity.com/tilly-shilling (*Accessed: March 2019*)

British Women's Racing Driver's Club (2018) *Members BARC race Beatrice Shilling* Available from: www.bwrdc.co.uk (*Accessed 2018*)

Brooklands (1939) *Last Race at Brooklands* Available from: www.brooklandsmuseum.com/explore/our-history/motor-racing (*Accessed: December 2018*)

Brooklands (c1930s) Poster – *Racing at Brooklands* Available from: www.brooklandsmuseum.com/explore/our-history/motor-racing *(Accessed: December 2018)*

BSA: (2018) *BSA Motorcycles* Available from: https://en.wikipedia.org/wiki/BSAmotorcycles *(Accessed: February 2019)*

Cameron Edward (1910) *The importance of a carburetor* in the New York Times Available from: www.nytimes.com/1910/10/16/archives/importance-of-carburetor-function-performed-to-properly-control-the.html *(Accessed: February 2019)*

Census of England and Wales (1911) *Residents of Sidney House (aka 4 Sidney Villas) the Shilling family and servants* Available from: www.ancestry.co.uk *(Accessed: March 2019)*

Channel 4 (2020) *Inside the Spitfire Factory* Available from: www.channel4.com/programmes/inside-the-spitfire-factory/on-demand/70073-005 *(Accessed: 27.10.20)*

Coventry University (2019) *Beatrice Shilling Building* Available from: www.spellermetcalfe.com/project/beatriceshillingbuilding *(Accessed: January 2019)*

Cryer AB (2018) *Beatrice Shilling Explained* Available from: https://everything.explained.today/Beatrice_Shilling/ *(Accessed: December 2018*

Dunbar Roger (2006) *Elva Jottings* Available from: www.elva.com/history/aug06-jottings02.html(Accessed: *December 2018)*

Farnborough Society (2020) *Beatrice Shilling Plaque* Available from:
https://thefarnboroughsociety.org.uk/ *(Accessed: October 2020 online and via Contact Form)*

Francis Frith (2019) *Waterlooville The Village 1906 (e-card photo)* Available from: www.francisfrith.com *(licence purchased 16.4.19)* *(Accessed: April 2019)*

Freudenberg Matthew (2003) *Negative Gravity: A life of Beatrice Shilling (Lagonda image p119, George Naylor p74, Beatrice pp 12, 29, Letters pp 59, 60 & 66, F1 car 121.* © *Dennis Lock Charlton Press: UK*

Gandhi Mahatma (2020) *Diversity Quotes* Available from: www.wisesayings.com/diversity-quotes *(Accessed December 2020)*

Gordano (2016) *Miss Shillings Orifice image* Available from: https://gordanohomefront.wordpress.com/2016/02/11/miss-shillings-orifice/ *(Accessed: March 2019)*

Grand Prix (2109) *Lella Lombardie* Available from: www.grandprix.com/gpe/drv-lomlel.html *(Accessed: April 2019)*

Harley-Davidson (2018) *Harley-Davidson Motorbikes* Available from: www.harley-davidson.com *(Accessed: March 2018 & January 2019)*

Holloway James (2020) *How-miss-shillings-orifice-helped-win-the-war/* Available from:www.damninteresting.com/ *(Accessed: November 2020)*

Hopper Grace (2020) *Computer Scientist & Rear Admiral* Available from: Wikipedia Foundation https://en.wikipedia.org/wiki/Grace_Hopper *(Accessed: 2018 and 2020)*

IET (2021) *Laura Wilson, Caroline Haslett & Margaret Partridge*
www.theiet.org/membership/library-archives/the-iet-
archives/ *(Accessed: 2021)*

Institution of Mechanical Engineers (2020) IWD 2020 *Highlight on
Beatrice* Shilling *Available from: IME*
https://imechearchive.wordpress.com *(Accessed: 2020)*

International Women's Day (2019/20) *#ChooseToChallenge 2021*
Available from: www.internationalwomensday.com
(Accessed: November 2020)

LAT Photographic Archive (1957) in Matthew Freudenberg (2003)
Negative Gravity A life of Beatrice Shilling p 119 Charlton
Publications: UK *(Accessed: November 2020)*

Lego (2017) *LegoWeDo2* Available from:
https://education.lego.com/(Accessed: Autumn 2017) LEGO
Lockdown support @ https://education.lego.com/en-gb/homeschool *(2021)*

Lewis Andrew (2019) *Beatrice's memorabilia and badges*
Available from: https;//antique-
collecting.co.uk/2015/08/06/beatrices-brooklands-badges-
sold/ *(Accessed: January 2019)*

Locke Dennis & Woodford David (1910 – 1980) *Beatrice Shilling and
family photographs* Available from: Dennis Locke *(brother-in-
law)* and David Woodford *(nephew)* *(Accessed: 2019 – 2020)*

Lovelace Ada (2018) *Ada Lovelace* Available from: Wikipedia
Foundation https://enWikipedia.org/wiki/adalovelace
(Accessed: 2018 - 2020)

McCarthy & Stone (2019) *Beatrice Shilling Building* Available from www.mccarthyandstone.co.uk/retirement-properties-for-sale/shilling-place/ *(Accessed: March 2019)*

McKay Feargal (2017) *the Giro d'Italia Alfonsina Strada* Available from: www.podiumcafe.com/book-corner/ *(Accessed: 2018)*

Matchless (2020) *Matchless Motorcycles* Available from: www.classic-british-motorcycles.com/matchless-motorcycles.html & www.matchlesslondon.com/blog *(Accessed: November 2020)*

Manchester University (2019) *Beatrice Shilling Scholarship* Available from: www.eee.manchester.ac.uk/study/undergraduate/fees-and-funding/ *(Accessed: January 2019)*

Manchester University (2015) *Beatrice Shilling – Engineer and Battle of Britain Heroine* Available from: https://www.manchester.ac.uk/discover/news/beatrice-shilling--engineer-and-battle-of-britain-heroine/ *(Accessed: November 2018)*

Marriott Roger (2020) *Meccano Magazine article on Beatrice winning a competition.* Available by e-mail & www.nzmeccano.com July/August 1921 *(Accessed: November 2020)*

Marshallsay JJ (2020) *Horndean Light Railway in Memories of Bygone Portsmouth* Available from: Facebook www.facebook.com/groups/366005550201426 *(Accessed: November 2020)*

Norton (2018) *Norton Commando* Available from: www.nortonmotorcycles.com *(Accessed: January 2019)*

Newman Cathy (2018) *Bloody Brilliant Women: The Pioneers, Revolutionaries and Geniuses Your History Teacher Forgot to Mention* London: Collins

Nuffield Theatre Southampton (2019) *Tilly and the Spitfires* (Showing Feb 2019) Available from: nstheatres.co.uk *(Accessed: January 2019)*

Oxley Mat (2018) *Speed*

Available from: https://matoxley.com/hardbacks/ *(Accessed: January 2019)*

Petersfield Post (2018) *Nostalgia: Hampshire has been at the heart of military history* Available from: www.petersfieldpost.co.uk *(Accessed: November 2018).*

Professor Mucklow (1954) *Institution of Mechanical Engineers in* Grace's Guide to British History. Available from: www.gracesguide.co.uk *(Accessed: January 2019)*

Reese Peter (2019) *Merlin Engine image 1942* Available from: www.thehistorypress.co.uk/articles/beatrice-tilly-shilling-celebrated-aeronautical-and-motorcycle-engineer *(Accessed 2019 and 2020)*

Richard (2020) *Image of Royal Enfield bike* Available from: www.facebook.com/RedDevilMotors *(Accessed: Sept.2020)*

Royal Holloway London University (2019) *The Beatrice Shilling Building named in her memory* Available from: https://stridetreglown.com/projects/the-beatrice-shilling-building-rhul/ *(Accessed: January 2019)*

j

Shilling Beatrice (2018) *Beatrice Shilling* Available from: Wikipedia
  Foundation en.wikipedia.org/wiki/Beatrice Shilling
  (Accessed: November 2018)

Surrey University (2017) *IWD Beatrice Shilling: Honorary PhD*
  Available from:
  https://blogs.surrey.ac.uk/archives/2017/03/08/internationa
  l-womens-day-the-inspirational-beatrice-shilling-2/
  (Accessed: 2019)

The News (2019) *Local inventor, engineer and racing driver,*
  Beatrice Shilling OBE Celebrated Available in *The News March 8th*
  2019 (Accessed: March 2019)

Waterlooville Library Staff (2019) *Commemoration Beatrice Shilling*
  in Havant Council News Available from: www.havant.gov.uk/
  Staff provided Information including:

  Nottingham Journal (Monday 01 November 1937, page 3)

  Meccano competition (1921)

  Portsmouth News (1938) Beatrice Shilling's Racing Win.
  (Accessed: March 2019)

Wetherspoon's Pub (2018) *The Tilly Shilling in Farnborough*
  Available from: www.jdwetherspoon.com *(Accessed: 2018)*

Winchester Heritage (2018) *Extraordinary Women of Hampshire*
  exhibition: Beatrice Shilling Available from:
  www.winchesterheritageopendays.org/blog/2018/9/17/extrao
  rdinary-women-of-hampshire *(Accessed: March 2019)*

Yousafazia Malala (2016) 11 *Inspiring gender equality quotes that*
  will leave you thinking Available from:
  www.womensweb.in/2016/06/ *(Accessed: January 2021)*

Acknowledgements:

David Woodford, Beatrice's nephew for providing the early photographs of the Shilling girls – much appreciated - along with some snippets about Beatrice that I was unaware of including her skills in being ambidextrous and her house named Carfield! Also for keeping in touch over the writing of this book. *I enjoy our e-mails.*

Dennis Lock, Beatrice's brother-in-law, for providing background information on George, Beatrice and her sisters Nora and Nancy as well as B's parents, her nieces, Janet and Marion and nephew David. Such kind words about his mother-in-law, Annie, who sounds a real gem – if only we all could have such a sweet mother-in-law! Thanks for permission to use the photographs etc., too. *What a treasure trove you have!*

Eric Jackson's family, especially Steve and his Mum, who provided information about the shop in the early days, but sadly only had family holiday snaps that Eric took and nothing on Sidney Villas in the 1900s. *It was so lovely to receive your help, thanks.*

Trish Earle & Denmead Book Club for reading my first few chapters and encouraging me to carry on writing. *THANK YOU ALL!*

Geoff and Roger for trailering their Manx bikes to the Forest of Bere pub for the photo shoot regardless of the weather that day. *You are both amazing! Thanks for the follow up chat, too, Geoff.*

Joan Foster for providing details about her niece, Judy Derisley, Beatrice's God-daughter; also *'Carfield'* and its concrete floor! *The confirmation was good to have.*

Peter Hurst from the TFS for your prompt contacting skills via The Farnborough Society (TFS) in forwarding my request to Joan in the first instance. *It is much appreciated, thank you.*

John Brooks from the Solent branch of the Norton Owners Club (NOC) for arranging a photo shoot with two rather elderly Manx bikes and their owners. *Wet but wonderful, thanks.*

Judy Derisley God-daughter of Beatrice. Comments available via The Spitfire Factory Ch4 *I have written to Judy for further details but as yet have not received a reply.*

Verity, from Waterlooville Library for her help in tracking down information on Beatrice and supplying the article from the Nottingham Journal etc. as well as the information about the Meccano competition. *Thank you so much for reading part of my first draft and encouraging me to continue with the book.*

Wendy Freudenberg, the wife of the late Matthew Freudenberg, for her chatty e-mails and information about her inspiring grandchildren – *one a male ballet dancer* – but also for putting me in touch with Beatrice's family. *An amazing feat!*

Richard & Ali Inskip for providing the setting at the Forest of Bere (FOB) for the NOC photo shoot – pity about the rain! The FOB hosts the meetings for the NOC in non-Covid times, as well as Denmead Book Club. *Great hosts at all times!*

BOOKS BY ELSIE O'NEILL

TRADITIONAL SKIPPING SONGS WITH JESSICA & GRANDMA

Jessica and Grandma have collaborated well during Lockdown to produce this superb skipping book. There are 80 plus traditional rhymes to involve children and adults of all ages in exercise and physical activities at home, in the playground or for PE at school. It encourages pupils to learn the rhymes whilst performing physical activity either individually or in pairs/groups.

The rhymes have great cross curricular links to history, English, geography and various cultural influences from not only the UK but other countries around the world.

The songs and exercises can be used as a warm up/cool down or as part of a main lesson in both primary and secondary schools.

In addition to PE schools are using it with the lunchtime supervisors to teach skipping and the accompanying songs. The children are enjoying it, knowing granny skipped along to some of them which encourages conversations with grandparents and other family members.

The You Tube channel with demonstrations is a fabulous added extra to support the teaching of the skipping steps and songs – a great idea. I will certainly be using it to teach my class of future Olympic winning skippers! A great warm-up prior to football and rugby for all ages.

EV's comments: *A brilliant resource for teachers, coaches and parents!*
OFSTED WILL LOVE SEEING IT IN ACTION!

The book has also been used in care/nursing homes to encourage the patients to relive their youth by singing the songs and recalling childhood memories – music helps here! Conversations are flowing, laughter is explosive, spontaneous and so natural; all skipping along nicely!

Available from Amazon.
Read the e-book for free if a Kindle member.

BEATRICE SHILLING: A GIRL WITH GRIT Tweens & Teens Edition is a much lighter version with links to Jessica, her special bike and determination to succeed at everything she does – just like Beatrice. Jessica tells the stories of both females, STEM and how it is being tackled in schools etc. as well as the urgent need for a more gender balanced world.

MRS PATTY PLUM HAD A BIG BLUE BUM!

Ted, a pupil, tells the tale of this incredible teacher and amazing school on World Book Day 2021 when

Hugh Bonneville and David Walliams popped in via Zoom.

He recalls their interactions and chats with the children during Q&A sessions and much more with both celebrities. Both have given permission to use these sessions verbatim along with images from Zoom in this book, as have parents. Some of Hugh's and David's secrets were given away, too!

Did you know that David treats himself to a biscuit after every chapter he writes? He was The Boy in The Dress! David enjoys Roald Dahl books and once dressed up as the BFG.

Hugh not only loves David's books, but played Mr Stink in the BBC TV drama, and every day spent an hour in make-up to create an image that was more tramp-like. The film crew would then take it in turns to flick food and gunk at him as well as 'snot' onto his beard! Hugh also avoids puddings at lunchtime while on set in case he falls asleep and has a snooze.

Mrs Plum
You've got a huge bum
And quite a big tum
Give up the cakes
And chew some gum!

Ted starts off by describing events around school and some of the marvellous things Mrs Plum does with her class. She is a wonderful teacher, jokes with the children and is always game for a laugh, especially about her big, blue and wobbly bum which incidentally had a mind of its own

Ted's Bottom Burp Dictionary provides a brief history of the word *fart* and supplies many alternatives and explanations from across the world.

However, the big dilemma of the day concerned Mrs Plum's big, blue bum. Did it ruin the photograph with David Walliams?

"All I could see was your bum and I was thinking it can't be the photo. Your bum is in front of my face."

Read the book to find out what happened at 3pm on World book Day with David Walliams and Mrs Plum's big blue bum.

I love it! Bottom burps, whizzpoppers and a big blue bum that obscured David Walliams' face! Education at its best: full of fun, frivolousness, a fabulous teacher and Hugh Bonneville aka Mr Stink reading and answering questions.

Tony Ashridge Author

GRANDMA'S DNA & OTHER STUFF

Jessica and Grandma have set out to discover more about their family history. In doing so, they investigate Grandma's DNA and gain quite a bit of knowledge about it, too.

Can you even say deoxyribonucleic acid? DNA is easier!

Was Grandma related to a Viking warrior who set sail for Scotland in a longboat prior to arriving in Ireland?

Is there a clue hiding in her brother's 'Viking finger' which requires amputation? Maybe not, but who knows!

Perhaps she was a distant relative of Boudicca and the Iceni tribe?

Look at that hair!

What has Africa got to do with any of it? *She is Irish!*

Grandma is certainly of Celtic origins, but there is more to her than her long, curly red hair and determined feminist nature which ensures equality for all that follow in her wake.

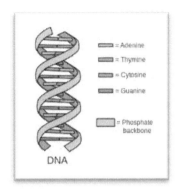

A FUTURE AMAZON PUBLICATION!

The current pipeline includes a book about

Carrie Morrison (1888 – 1950)

1922 saw her as the first English female solicitor who was very much a poor man's lawyer providing pro bono or low fee services to people in the East End of London at Toynbee Hall.

Explore her life from birth to 1950 and how she went from a teacher to a solicitor and everything in between. *Was she a spy?*

Available Spring 2022

ABOUT THE AUTHOR

I grew up in Belfast during the 1950s and 1960s. There were six children in total, the youngest being 19 years younger than me! (Viking finger man!)

We played in the street, on the field or went to the park. Street games, especially skipping and rounders, were a big part of my life and I have never forgotten those times. I loved the rhymes, the friends I skipped with and the body it gave me – I was tall, skinny, fit and healthy.

As children we had many shared bikes. Mum's red racer was a favourite as was the Triang three-wheeler with a lidded boot which we raced against my brother in his wheelchair. We had scooters, too.

I adore lasagne, mangoes, decaf tea, Veda Bread and Granny's Irish chicken and vegetable broth with freshly made bread. *I am no longer skinny!*

My husband and I, (*I sound like the Queen*) enjoy the odd holiday, mostly cruising to exotic destinations. My favourites include: the UAE, China, Australia, the Caribbean and Japan. Fortunately, we missed the Covid-19 outbreak on the Diamond Princess in Yokohama as it came a few months after our return to the UK. It was very sad watching the ship docked in Japan with so many people infected on board. A very difficult time for passengers, staff and the cruise industry itself. Although I love to travel, I am a home bird at heart. We should have been cruising around the British Isles with the ship docking in Belfast, but the Corona Virus has put paid to that along with Lockdown.

Perhaps we might be able to do it in a year's time. However, being safe is crucial and I am staying in!

Hampshire is an amazing place to live and work: I love our village, but I have never forgotten my roots in Belfast and Co. Down, Northern Ireland.

Millisle, Ballycopeland, Ballywalter and Donaghadee were very important to me as all our school holidays were spent with Granny and Grandad who lived right on the beach in Millisle.

We would fish, swim, even if wet, take boats out, climb the rocks and collect dulse, an edible seaweed, to dry on the shed roof. It cost 3d a bag if bought locally but we enjoyed wading out to the dulse rocks during low tide and having it for free. Sadly a skill or experience none of my children or grandchildren are likely to have.

We made sand houses reinforcing the seats with slates and collected bottles to get the penny deposit back from The First & Last pub. The money was spent on ice cream and Benny's amusements.

Our cousins lived nearby – *'up the road towards Ballycopeland'* and a few miles away in Donaghadee, but we also met people from many destinations in the UK, Europe and America.

Millisle was a sought after holiday resort with families coming for the month of August or a week in a caravan. We'd walk for miles, play ball and board games, cards, skip and read for hours on end. *Reading is something I still do daily.*

Millisle was absolute Heaven for eight weeks every summer. The memories are unforgettable. Thank you, Granny & Granddad. RIP

We loved it!

Elsie O'Neill

AFTERWORD

Many thanks for reading my second book
Beatrice Shilling OBE: A Dame with Determination!

I first came across Beatrice while teaching and exploring WWII with my Year 3/4s in Hampshire many years ago. They absolutely adored the topic. A wonderful reconstruction was our *'evacuation'* by train to another school in the city, where we carried out wartime activities including writing postcards home and drama as the bombs hit. Dressed in wartime style outfits and carrying *'gas masks'* as well as an *'authentic'* packed lunch wrapped in greaseproof paper, we were admired and questioned by many as we walked to the station. Beatrice was born a few miles away. Sadly she wasn't known locally.

I felt it was important to get Beatrice's achievements in the public domain but didn't believe a traditional history book would necessarily appeal to the Tweens and Teens who are our future. Hence writing my earlier book: *Beatrice Shilling: A Girl with Grit* linking Jessica's determination, love of bikes, musical theatre and water sports as well as television and internet work to appeal.

Our children must be proud of their accomplishments without being conceited or arrogant. STEM exploration and teaching is essential for both boys and girls and we need to encourage it to ensure we develop the right technology and expertise within the UK and across the world. *Female participation is crucial.*

Equal opportunities and gender issues require addressing too. They were problematic one hundred years ago and shouldn't be in 2021.

Nature or nurture is a difficult one. However, families and educators need to guarantee we provide ample STEM type experiences equally to boys and girls.

Adults must learn, too!

https://educationtechnologysolutions.com/2019/03/science-technology-engineering-arts-mathematics/
©Jane Hunter reddit.com

Australia is forging ahead and including the Arts, too, as is the case in some schools in the UK. This needs to be more widespread and encompassed in our curriculum from pre-school to university levels.

Our world needs those skills to compete globally. *Teach now!*

Printed in Great Britain
by Amazon

75340071R10090